The Christian
And The Occult

The Christian And The Occult

Roger C. Palms

The Wheel Of Fortune

JUDSON PRESS
Valley Forge

THE CHRISTIAN AND THE OCCULT

Bible quotations in this volume are in accordance with the Revised Standard Version of the Bible, copyright 1946 and 1952 by the Division of Christian Education of the National Council of the Churches of Christ in the United States of America, and are used by permission.

Library of Congress Cataloging in Publication Data

Palms, Roger C
    The Christian and the occult.

    Includes bibliographical references.

    1. Christianity and occult sciences. I. Title.

BR115.03P35   133   72-652
ISBN 0-8170-0569-2

Printed in the U.S.A.

Contents

1. Secrets from the Night 7

2. The Aquarian Age 16

3. The Awakening Past 25

4. The Church:
A Flickering Light 35

5. The Spreading Craft 46

6. Rulers of the Shadows 81

7. The God of This World 94

8. "I Saw Satan Fall Like
Lightning from Heaven" 105

Author's Postscript 124

1
Secrets from the Night

A quiet "Blessed Be!" passes between two people as they slip out of their neighbor's home late at night. They are brothers in witchcraft wishing each other well until their next sabbat.

"And so it is," ends a prayer to the "Presence" in a Science of Mind church service. The worshipers leave "programmed" with a new thought for the week.

"Hail, Satan, Our Lord and Master," is chanted by hundreds in a dark room; another petition has been offered by people who have given themselves as a "living sacrifice" to Satan.

"Wait a minute," says a twentieth-century skeptic. "You can't tell me that civilized people still practice witchcraft or really put faith in those metaphysical thought patterns or worship Satan. That sort of thing went out with the witch-hunts nearly three hundred years ago!"

But when the skeptic who says that reads his newspaper or talks to the teenager next door or looks in the window of the new bookstore on the corner or notices the many late night visitors at the house across the street, he begins to find out that he is wrong. The religions of the occult are rapidly spreading everywhere.

While her two children sleep, a young woman steps out of her ritualistic salt water bath and "sky clad" (nude) joins her husband and eleven others in the basement of her Long Island home. There she draws a nine-foot circle on the floor with a 400-year-old sword. All thirteen witches enter the circle to begin the ancient ritual of a Halloween night sabbat.

In a cemetery near Daytona Beach six unearthed graves reveal bodies without heads. The skulls have been used in a midnight witches' ceremony.

On the morning following a nighttime invasion of English graveyards, stories in the British press tell of desecrated graves, broken crosses, opened coffins, and the remains of a witches' gathering. The next night still other small town English cemeteries are invaded. A person schooled in the black arts says that the desecration is part of a devil worship ritual and that it is increasing everywhere.

In a deserted house in Michigan's Livingston County, a seventeen-year-old girl is found brutally tortured and slain. The two charged with the killing are described as members of an occult group called "Satan's Satanic Servants."

According to press reports, the women arrested in the gruesome 1969 Sharon Tate murders obeyed Charles Manson as "god" and "satan." Their victims' mutilated bodies were carved with "X" marks, a black magic sign.

When Patrick Michael Newell was killed in Vineland, New Jersey, his companions told police that they killed him at his own request. Newell had said that he expected to return to earth as a leader of Satan's devils.

Two recent murder victims in Montana and California were found dismembered. Both slayers confessed to being Satan worshipers.

On July 25, 1968, a life-size effigy of a woman was found near England's Newberry Common. According to the *Daily Mail,* it was used in a pagan fertility rite.

"It really works!" Those were the words of an excited prison inmate who made a pact with Satan to prevent his trial by a particularly severe judge. Shortly after the pact was made, the judge fell, breaking a hip. The prisoner was tried by a milder judge, received a lighter sentence, and is delighted with the power of Satan that is at his disposal.

A teenager in the Midwest wanted to get rid of a troublesome schoolmate. So she cast an ancient spell by burying a potato near her house while chanting certain words. Each night she dug up the potato and reburied it a few feet farther away. In a few days the unwanted student stopped coming around.

A young male witch whose father is a minister says he sold his soul to the Devil when he was ten years old. But, he said, he prayed about it first.

At Michigan State University, one co-ed requested an immediate room change when her roommate brought friends in for a naked orgy. Her roommate claimed to be a witch.

At a recent Los Angeles witchcraft convention, twenty firms pushed their occult wares. Hundreds of people came to enlarge their personal stock of occult supplies. "People are buying the freakier stuff," said a witch who sells the strange occult items that people seem to want the most.

On Berkeley's Telegraph Avenue, Isaac Bonewits, with an earned bachelor's degree in magic from the University of California, plies his trade. "He'll cast a spell for you for a price," explains a Berkeley resident.

Across the Bay on California Street in San Francisco, Anton Szandor LaVey, founder of the Church of Satan, conducts worship purposely intended to stimulate human lust. LaVey, who enjoys the title "Black Pope," claims 10,000 dues-paying members in his church. They pay to worship Satan in LaVey's totally black house, offering praise to the Devil as "lord."

Time magazine, June 19, 1972, describes a U.S. Army officer who is a fourth-degree satanist priest, a member of the Satanic Church "Council of Nine," the editor of Anton LaVey's paper the *Cloven Hoof,* and the author of "a widely used ROTC textbook."

At a large midwestern university, a co-ed approached the librarian and asked where she could find books about witches.

"What do you want to know about witches?" asked the librarian.

"I want to know how to become one!"

The occult is growing. According to *Newsweek,* August 16, 1971:

> . . . today tens of thousands across the U.S.—some of them middle-class adults with advanced university degrees—are dabbling in Satanism, witchcraft, voodoo and other forms of black or white magic. . . . But a good deal of the arcane experimentation results from plain blind faith in Satanic power, which sometimes produces macabre acts of violence and sex. . . .

Billy Graham, on a crusade telecast November 29, 1971, said, "Eighty percent of the young people in Great Britain have been in touch with witches and wizards."

According to *Time* magazine, June 19, 1972, German journalist Horst Knaut has estimated that "at least 3,000,000 West Germans subscribe to some form of the occult."

In 1971, James Guthrie, who heads the Church of Satan in Los Angeles, led a "Crusade for Satan" in major American cities.

Once limited to the superstitions of uneducated people, and practically unknown since the end of the Salem witch trials, the religions of the occult are once again attracting unprecedented numbers of Western people.

ESP (Extrasensory perception), clairvoyance, clairaudience, telekinesis, visiting mediums, the use of tarot cards, astral projection, astrology, numerology, white and black witchcraft, satanism, ouija boards, and spiritualism are capturing the minds of young and old alike.

The occult is big business. Twelve hundred of the 1,750 daily newspapers in the United States carry columns on astrology, according to a *Time* magazine study. An astrological forecast is now available to help stock market investors make profitable decisions.

Using computers, *Time Pattern Research Institute, Inc.*, told *Time* magazine reporters it could turn out 10,000 word horoscope readings in two minutes for a total of 10,000 horoscopes a month.

Judy Klemesrud, in an October 31, 1969, *New York Times* article, wrote that witch Sybil Leek claims one thousand people each week tell her that they are either interested in witchcraft or want to become witches.

Susy Smith, whose book *Today's Witches* [1] speaks of love spells, drug rituals, devil worship, sex rites, and secret societies, estimates that there are 60,000 witches in the United States. The high priest of Michigan witches disagrees. He claims that there are 200,000 practicing witches in the United States.

The *Berkeley Barb* carries advertising for Astrologer Samantha featured daily Monday through Friday on KSAN-FM 95 radio. She discusses listeners' problems over the air.

In an upstairs office on San Francisco's busy Powell Street, the Metaphysical Library offers "Healing treatment, E.S.P., and Astrology Solving All Problems."

Entropy, of San Francisco, offers free university courses in astrology: casting and interpreting, learning to read and understand the tarot, and an encounter group using the *yin* and *yang* theory of *I Ching*.

---

[1] Susy Smith, *Today's Witches* (Englewood Cliffs, N.J.: Prentice-Hall, Inc., 1970; paperback edition. Award Books).

San Francisco's Bay Area Center for Alternative Education offers courses in astrology, tarot, ceremonial magic, and witchcraft.

Housewives going through the check-out stand of their favorite supermarket can pick up *Everyday Witchcraft*, a 25¢ Dell purse book which tells them in simple language how to work with love magic, charms, spells, fortune telling, and "everything you need to know to enjoy occult power!" The provocative cover tells the interested woman that if she dares to, she can arouse a man's desire, torment an enemy, decide her baby's sex, and keep a man faithful. Louise Huebner, the well-known Los Angeles witch, has written nine such mini-books for the 1972 Hallmark spring book line.

A Cleveland firm offers a witch rental service for parties, and a book club selling occult books has built up a 100,000 member business in two years.

"Barbara the Gray Witch" and other popular occult-type records sell in large numbers to teenagers.

Russian scientists are deeply involved in the study of psychic phenomena. Government-sponsored research is testing ways to move objects without touching them (psychokinesis).

A recent NASA moon mission included attempts at sending telepathic messages to Earth.

In England, witches still claim to be responsible for saving their homeland from Hitler's planned invasion. They say that their "cone of power," a spell cast across the Channel, kept Hitler off British soil.

Many Christians who laughed at Satan as a cartoon figure with horns and a red suit or who enjoyed the beautiful blonde witch on television are now discovering that the occult is not a funny game or superstition. It is no longer the religion of the few, but it is attracting thousands, even capturing many who claim to be trusting in Jesus Christ as Savior and Lord.

The occult is deceptive. People, convinced that it is Christian, or at least religious, are drawn into it because they are fooled by the use of familiar Bible quotations or religious terminology.

Susy Smith, in *Today's Witches*, tells of three church-going "Christians" who prayed to the Lord Jesus to kill the husband of one of the women. They took seriously the words of Jesus "where two or three are gathered together in my name," and agreed to ask that the unappreciated husband die. He did—of a heart attack.[2]

2 Susy Smith, *op. cit.*, pp. 105-106.

Before each seance one "Christian" group, led by an ex-minister, begins with the Lord's Prayer, sets the tone for the experience with the singing of "Have Thine Own Way, Lord," and prepares for the visitation of spirits with the song "In the Garden," because they say it has a message about spirit visitation.

"I believe in Jesus," said a psychic in California. She added, "Jesus is the way into the world of the supernatural." And to prove her point, she misquoted Jesus: "And greater things than this shall ye do, for you shall be as gods."

"Jesus has the oldest and most evolved spirit," explained a spiritualist. "Each one of us can and will become a Jesus someday. We, too, will carry God's truth to another planet of a lower sphere just as Jesus did when he came to this earth."

"Jesus was the greatest medium," explained another spiritualist. "We need to become like Jesus."

"Jesus was a witch. After all, didn't he have a coven?" According to this particular witch, Jesus and his disciples made the special "13," the number of persons in a witches' coven.

Jesus held a "seance" on the Mount of Transfiguration, according to David N. Bubar, a former Southern Baptist pastor who now heads the Spiritual Outreach Society. In an interview for *Home Missions,* a Southern Baptist publication, he said, "Jesus communicated with Moses and Elijah. . . ." Then he added, "Furthermore, Jesus communicated with the dead when he raised Lazarus. . . ." [3]

"Jesus Christ? Oh, yes," said a student of reincarnation. "He is the 'Christ principle.' It's by the 'Christ principle' that we are able to move from one incarnation into another until the time when we are able to come into complete harmony with God."

People in various forms of religious science are told: "Christ incarnates into different people. He did it to Jesus, then left him at age thirty."

Another religious-science group teaches, "The divinity is linked to man by his mind."

"Why do you say 'Divinity,' not God?" asks a Christian.

"Not God, because we created God in our own image. We can call God by many names, whether Allah or God or universal spirit—it doesn't matter. We reach out toward God with a mind link; the mind is the vehicle for reaching."

[3] *Home Missions* (January, 1972), p. 19.

"Jesus is a living vibration," a psychic teaches.

"Jesus taught a new birth," says another. "Christians believe in the new birth, and that's what we believe in, too. It's very clear what Jesus meant by the new birth—every spirit chooses his next parents, and his date of birth, so that he can arrive on this earth under the right sign prepared to learn the next lessons needed for his journey toward God."

A spokesman for Spiritual Frontiers Fellowship, teaching "new life" and a continuous life hereafter, told a teenage audience that SFF was created to bring the psychic back into the church. He noted that the program which started in Illinois in 1956 now has chapters in all fifty states. It sponsors conferences and seminars to lead church people into an understanding of psychic phenomena. With a membership of over six thousand, every lecture and conference brings still more new members.

The Spiritual Frontiers Fellowship application form says members are interested in spiritual healing, prayer and meditation, psychic communication and survival, and psychic research "as a means to spiritual development." The SFF, which has always boasted a clergyman as president, is "dedicated to the expansion of consciousness toward the realization of Man's intrinsic spiritual nature," according to the membership application.

"But do you believe in the Trinity?" asked a man in the audience of an SFF lecture.

"Yes, I do," replied the speaker of the evening. "I understand the Trinity, too—it's you, me, and God."

Occult people like to use the Bible. Dr. Moses Hull, in his book *Biblical Spiritualism*, refers to the Bible as a sacred book and teaches that the apostle Paul received a spirit revelation from Jesus, who served as a medium.[4]

"Of course I believe in the Bible as the divinely inspired word of God," said a spokesman from the Psychic Research Foundation in Chicago. "And I believe in the Koran . . ." he said, and he named many other religious books.

"It's biblical to use tarot cards," said one occult believer. "John, in the twenty-two chapters of his Book of Revelation, describes the twenty-two cards of the Major Arcana. Chapters four and five de-

---

[4] Moses Hull, *Encyclopedia of Biblical Spiritualism* as quoted by Victor Ernest, *I Talked with the Spirits* (Wheaton, Ill.: Tyndale House Publishers, 1971), p. 43.

scribe the wheel of fortune, ten tells of the temperance card, and twelve describes the Empress."

Acts 8:26-30 proves the place of spiritualism in the Bible, according to one spiritualist. He explained that Philip "was carried by a control spirit" to the place where he met the Ethiopian eunuch.

A college girl, who left satanism when she accepted Jesus Christ as her Savior and Lord, quoted the "Bible" verse she had to learn. "I beseech you, therefore, brethren by Satan, to give your bodies as a living sacrifice to Satan, which is your spiritual service of worship."

Most occult people think of themselves as very religious. "ESP and the study of psychic phenomena, even astrology, should be dedicated to God," says a psychic teacher who tries to balance faith in Christ with a quest for the mystical.

When Alex Sanders, an English witch, was interviewed by June Johns for her book *King of the Witches,* he told her that witchcraft and Christianity were compatible.[5]

A Spiritual Frontiers Fellowship brochure quotes Chaplain Howard C. Wilkinson's teaching that "extrasensory communication regularly takes place between God and man." In other words, the brochure explains, "prayer is telepathic." This extrasensory communication can also make contact with other souls that have gone over to "the other side."

An evangelistic gospel team, ministering to churches in the Midwest, stresses astrology as the best way to understand oneself and one's potential. After presenting a gospel message, they talk to people about astrology.

According to *Newsweek,* August 16, 1971, young evangelists of the Church of the Final Judgment have been proselytizing on the streets of Boston and New York. They are seeking converts to their religion which worships both Christ and Satan.

The Reverend Arthur Ford, called America's foremost psychic medium, had among his clients the late Episcopal Bishop James A. Pike. In his book *The Other Side,* Pike described his communication with his dead son.[6] Pike is only one of many ministers

---

[5] June Johns, *King of the Witches: The World of Alex Sanders* (New York: Coward, McCann and Geoghegan, Inc., 1970), p. 121.

[6] See James A. Pike, *The Other Side* (New York: Dell Publishing Company, Inc., 1969).

who claim to have found in the mystical religions of the occult some of the answers that they missed in their churches.

One Protestant minister found that he was able to handle funerals better when he came to believe in spiritualism. Then he "knew" that there was life after death.

"It's a beautiful age," according to a speaker at a Detroit meeting of Spiritual Frontiers Fellowship. "We are drawing to the conclusion of the Piscean age, the age introduced by Jesus, and coming into the age of Aquarius."

"It's going to be splendid because people who are investigating their (psychic) experiences and teaching them to their children will raise their children to also seek in the psychic realms. It will be a harmonious, seeking - developing - glorious time," said an enthusiastic believer in psychic religion.

Committed Christians need to hear what the growing numbers in the occult religions are saying. Occult people are excited about a new age, an age that has "outgrown" Jesus Christ.

"It's thrilling," says a believer in Mind Science. "My church is jammed with young people who are expanding their consciousnesses and are learning to live life on a level of spiritual consciousness. This is good!"

Satanism is an answer to "repressive" Judeo-Christian teachings. According to Anton LaVey, people in other churches are eager to get their worship over with so that they can start enjoying themselves. In the Satan churches, people celebrate their bodies and carnal desires.

A British high priestess in witchcraft told newspaper reporters that witchcraft will overtake Christianity by the turn of the century.

"The church is shaking now," says Henry Rucker, Director of the Psychic Research Foundation in Chicago. In his lecture to teenagers, Rucker, who is introduced as a palmist, spiritual healer, medium, clairvoyant, and clairaudient, says, "Aquarians are clicking on every day, talking about the past life and vibrations. They are coming in with love, healing people with Aquarian music, and God is doing it through them."

Another psychic adds, "During the Aquarian age we will find ourselves in a new way implementing love, evolving spiritually, becoming more human, becoming more psychic."

According to them, the Age of Aquarius is dawning.

2 The Aquarian Age

Sally Eaton of *Hair,* a popular Broadway musical that boasts a staff astrologer in the program credits, sings about the dawning of the Age of Aquarius. The song is full of optimism and hope.

For thousands of people it is the end of the Christian or Piscean era and the beginning of the Aquarian Age, the age of the water bearer. Believers in the metaphysical and the occult say the new age has been predicted for one hundred years, has been dawning for almost seventy years, and will last for 2,600 years.

Astrologer Carroll Righter told *Time* magazine reporters (March 21, 1969): "The Piscean Age was an age of tears and sorrow, focused on the death of Christ. In 1904, we entered the Age of Aquarius, which will be an age of joy, of science and accomplishment, focused on the life of Christ."

And, if Edgar Cayce, the well-known psychic, and Jeane Dixon, noted for predicting the death of President Kennedy, are correct, this new age will see the kingdoms of this world united under a great leader who was born in 1962. He will bring peace and hope before he shows himself to be the anti-Christ.

Many observers of the mood of the times have noted that Western man has become so baffled by the very complex social and economic problems that he has lost his faith in scientific reason and is increasingly attracted to the kind of irrational solutions offered by the occult.

During the age of scientism, it was assumed that man was either religious or scientific. "Now we know," explained a university

16

religion professor, "that the alternative to religion is not rationalism; it is superstition."

The occult is coming out into the open. People who secretly practiced clairvoyance, visited a palmist, or studied their astrological charts behind closed doors are now openly talking about it. Others are eagerly listening to what they say. The occult is attractive. People are seeking it because it seems to work.

Witches' covens are forming. Schools for the training of witches are being set up around the country, some through occult bookstores, others as free university-type courses. Some people are beginning to explore witchcraft and psychic phenomena through legitimate universities and colleges.

Psychiatrist Carl G. Jung was quoted in *Time* magazine, March 21, 1969, as stating: "Today, rising out of the social deeps, astrology knocks at the doors of the universities, from which it was banished some 300 years ago."

Bowling Green State University recently offered students a course in mysticism and occultism.

In Maryland, the press reports that Department of Education officials are giving consideration to the establishment of the country's first accredited school of esoteric arts and sciences at Aquarian University of Maryland. The abbreviation of the school letters, AUM, is a Hindu chant meaning "one with God."

A San Diego Christian newspaper reports that San Diego State College is funding an experimental college course in witchcraft.

Time magazine, March 21, 1969, reported that 247 people registered for a non-credit course in witchcraft offered by the University of South Carolina. The *New York Times,* October 31, 1969, listed both the University of South Carolina and the University of Alabama as offering courses in witchcraft. The *Times* on June 1, 1969, reported that when students at a Canadian university were given a chance to recommend courses to be included in the curriculum, they picked sorcery, witchcraft, Zen, and astrology.

A Michigan mother was alarmed to learn that witchcraft was being offered to interested students at the local high school.

Andrew M. Greeley, writing in the *New York Times* on June 1, 1969, described the "Women's International Terrorists Corps from Hell" (WITCH). Claiming to worship the mother earth goddess, this group of women from the University of Chicago tried to put a curse on one of their professors. In the same article, Greeley reported an interview with an M.I.T. professor who said that his seminar material on occult religions was not just studied but practiced by the students. He described them as high scoring, Ivy League, aristocratic kids.

The occult is growing fastest among the young. "There has to be a system of beliefs to cling to," said a Michigan State University co-ed who calls herself a believing witch. She added, "Machines would ruin our lives; this is a way of getting back into focus with nature. People close to nature are close to the forces. There is power here, power for us to reserve and channel."

"Man is a microcosm of the macrocosm," said a student of astrology. He explained, "What happens in the stars happens in man."

"It's a fitting together," said a young witch.

The occult is a surrogate for religion. It gives man what he doesn't find in the established religions. Established religions teach God, say the witches. Witchcraft teaches a "life spirit." "The occult makes me one with the whole," said a witch. "I am one with God."

Many people in the occult believe that as the astronauts probe outer space and other scientists probe the very secrets of minutia, man must also look into the depths of his own being. To them, man needs to discover himself and the cosmos. Occult beliefs offer a way of coming to an understanding of the human universe as a part of the larger cosmic universe.

Young people who once discovered some of these "new dimensions" through the use of mind-expanding drugs are now seeking the same experiences through expanding psychic consciousness. They are turning from drugs to the occult.

The occult, like drugs, weakens ego boundaries. It opens up a group mind feeling that "we are all one." Space and time concepts are altered, enhancing clairvoyance and other psychic experiences.

"Drugs opened my mind to a dimension that I had not known before," said one occult seeker. He explained that there is more to this world than our senses reveal. There are feelings and there is power. People who once found excitement in looking outward to the explanations of science are finding answers by looking inward to the discovery of the power inside themselves.

When Carlos Castaneda published *The Teachings of Don Juan:*

A Yaqui Way of Knowledge, it became a best seller among the young. Don Juan spoke of "feeling" the world around him. He taught "seeing" by entering into seeing and being with his whole nature.[1] This whole sensation experience is being sought by many people. It is this desire to "know" through the whole consciousness that leads people into the occult.

"Do you want to know why I've gone into witchcraft?" asked a witch. "For the same reason that the Jesus freaks have gone into Jesus. They find their hope in Jesus—I find power in the occult."

"It is personal to me, whereas so many other aspects of life are not," said a member of an occult group.

Alvin Toffler in *Future Shock* describes this feeling as a longing for community.[2] Some members of the occult find their community in communes. And what they find sounds very much like the togetherness that Christ designed the church to offer Christians.

Using words that sound descriptive of the Christian fellowship, Dr. Stephen E. Beltz, former executive director of Philadelphia's Center for Behavior Modification, told Adon Taft of the Miami *Herald,* December 24, 1971, that communes offer "a warmth and open expression of true and honest feelings."

There are nearly a quarter of a million people living in more than 30,000 communes in the United States. Many of these practice occult religions.

Some of the intentional communities or communes studied by Stanley Krippner, Director of the Dream Laboratory, Maimonides, Brooklyn, are based on a life-style that includes telepathy, clairvoyance, and other pyschokinetic activities. He reports communes involved in astral travel, altered consciousness, paranormal communication, tarot card readings to determine the future, astrology charts to help in planting crops, and the use of *I Ching.*[3]

Even the people who were involved in the "Whole Earth View" seem to be giving way to "Place," a concept of "knowing where

[1] Carlos Castaneda, "Further Conversations with Don Juan" in *Esquire* magazine, March, 1971, pp. 75 ff. See also Carlos Castaneda, *The Teachings of Don Juan: A Yaqui Way of Knowledge* (Berkeley: University of California Press, 1968, and New York: Ballantine Books, Inc., 1971).

[2] See Chapter 6 of Alvin Toffler, *Future Shock* (New York: Random House, Inc., 1970).

[3] Stanley Krippner, "Mystic Communes," in *The Modern Utopian.*

you are." James A. Finefrock wrote in the March 19, 1972, issue of the *San Francisco Examiner and Chronicle*, quoting Dudley De Zonia, "Place is a step from tools to consciousness, a kind of consciousness that involves the awe, love, ingenuity, and spiritual need connecting a person to a place."

Believers in the occult feel that through the occult man can find his role and place in the world. The natural laws of this world are governed by the cosmos. The moon affects the waves of the sea; the pull of the sun affects the earth; gravity controls the planets; and thus occult followers believe that all of these forces work together to affect man. The occult is a way of trying to work with and understand the principles that operate within the world and beyond it.

The occult is very religious. It has room for all of the other religions of the world. To occult people no religion is wrong and no one way is absolutely right. All are ways of discovering human potential and moving toward the fulfillment of a person in the "Ultimate," which to them is God.

The extra-normal or supernatural dimensions of man tended to be ignored by the psychology of the 1930's and 1940's. Educated men were given to believe that the five senses offered the only source for knowledge and experience; there was nothing else. Belief in the supernatural was written off as somewhat "unenlightened." But this rationalism left many people empty. Today there is a feeling about "knowing" that convinces people that there is more to man than the experiences that come from measurable causes or physical actions.

Dreams that come true, a sense of an aura around certain people, objects being moved by thought or breaking at a certain moment, and similar thoughts in the minds of two people in the same room or many miles apart are all indications of other dimensions of a person and his world.

"You all have met someone, perhaps in a crowded room or on a bus, and have just known that you knew him before," said a psychic. "That's because you knew him in another life."

"There's more to me than man can measure scientifically," says the psychic. An increasing number of people fully agree with him. For some, this turning inward is a searching for the transcendence of God on human terms. The otherness of God, his omnipotence and transcendence, seems to have disappeared from the teachings of many Christian churches as they become more and more involved in numbers, buildings, programs, and finances. Yet, at the same time, people have been longing for Someone larger than themselves.

Even the gospel message, with its personal theme, has sometimes been presented in a way that overlooks the transcendence and holiness of the living God who came to this earth in Christ Jesus. The lack of awe for God leaves people with a longing for the supernatural.

There is a feeling, according to such writers as Jacob Needleman in *The New Religions,* that many people who reject Christianity do so because the Christian faith, or at least the proclaimers of Western Christianity, have ignored the universality and otherness of God.[4] They feel that as important as personal belief and action are, man's dependency on nature must be taught and the universe needs to be emphasized as part of the whole picture of man's relationship to God.

The nature religions and the religions of the occult that stress the power of the earth and the God of the cosmos and the harmony of man with nature are popular today. They call the Christian to take another look at the biblical aspects of a natural theology. Christians need to expand their teaching to include the concept of man existing within a cosmos that God has ordained. And they need to stress the natural order as important to God and to themselves.

In a mass-media, noisy, materialistic age there is a longing for self-awareness, a seeking for the inner soul as it relates to the whole of God's order. There is a searching for oneness with the inner dimensions of another person and with the secrets of nature. When occult seekers meet a Christian who ignores this need in them, they assume that Christianity deals only with a church relationship, and they go on looking within the occult for answers to their quest for universal relationships.

Christians are poor disciples when they ignore this longing of people to meet the transcendent and yet very present living God. It is a poor witness to present Christ only as the Savior from sin and not also as the Savior for life and wholeness.

Today as people, particularly the young, move away from scien-

[4] Jacob Needleman, *The New Religions* (Garden City, N.Y.: Doubleday & Company, Inc., 1970), p. 4.

tism, commercialism, and all of the things that once influenced and controlled man, they are beginning to look inside and around them for a harmony within themselves, with the universe and the soil. For many this harmony is found in an ecological love of the simple and the clean. Others are seeking after "good vibrations" from spirits, the cosmos, and other people. Realizing that there is a greater dimension and power in man than they ever recognized before, they are looking for ways to enlarge that power.

Some are simply seeking power. Young witches have frankly admitted that it is a lot easier to cast a spell to win a boyfriend or a good grade in school than it is to work for them. But others are finding in the occult the discipline that they have found lacking in life but have always wanted. They find a commitment to rules and ritual, and an excitement from the vibrations of love, music, and other people.

Every alert campus minister knows that students are asking personal faith questions. They are looking for guidance. One Christian told his campus chaplain, "If I'm going to bring a non-Christian to any of our meetings, I'll bring him to our prayer meeting where he can feel the love of the people for each other and know that they really trust God to answer prayer and intervene in the important issues of their lives."

In a dormitory of a large midwestern university a group of students were intently hunched over a Ouija board.

"Oh, yes," said a woman who heard about the Ouija board. "That was a parlor game when I was young, too."

But to those students, it is no parlor game. They are seriously seeking guidance for their lives and answers to their problems. They, like the praying young Christians a few doors away, want a faith that works.

A Christian explained that the attraction to the occult cannot be written off simply as "mystical" or a little "naughty." People are drawn to it because they have seen that it brings results for the people who practice it. Results and commitment in a Christian's life will draw the same seeking people. Words alone will not.

Just as a Christian message that is strictly "man centered" doesn't satisfy the occult people who are oriented to the universe, the study of the universe from a scientific standpoint doesn't satisfy them either. The study of biology or chemistry or the nature of man, including psychology, doesn't help man to understand his personal relationship to creation. The wholeness of man within the wholeness of nature is what so many practitioners of the occult are seeking.

The longing for good vibrations is causing a religious quest that leads people to investigate and embrace spiritualism, witchcraft, astrology, and even Satan worship. There is a mystery to life and a mystery to God. Many want to know what that mystery is. Christians know that when man ignores the revelation of God about himself, he will supply his own answers to those mysteries from some other source. The vibrations sought and found by Aquarians fill that seeking void. Through the occult they feel that they belong. They have an explanation for their very being. They have power, and it feels good.

When man reaches out to the occult, he is not merely adapting witchcraft to a mechanized Western society. He is not simply trying to find a pragmatic way of working out his life through spells or the use of ESP or telekinesis or astrology. He is reaching back to the roots of his own history to find his source. Through the occult many hope to find themselves and to find God.

The fact that people move in these directions, seeking answers about God, man, and the universe while ignoring the revelation of God shows the pressure of Satan upon them. Satan does what he has always done to keep people away from the wholeness available in Jesus Christ. He disguises the truth and counterfeits the gifts and blessings of God. He gives artificially and temporarily what God gives permanently in Christ.

Although some occult worshipers have gone totally to the extreme of worshiping Satan, they are still the exception. Most people in the occult have not gone as far as pure satanism. But Satan knows that he can still possess them. He doesn't need everyone to be his outwardly committed servant. Good people who "worship" God by the guidance and the direction of Satan are far more useful to him than the extreme satanist. They are also far more attractive to others. They are the ones whom he deceives in order to make their lives a deceiving witness.

The rise of the occult points to a searching in man. He is asking age-old questions. What are the forces that draw and control and push his life? How is this package of body, mind, and spirit put together? What is it that makes a person uniquely himself? "Why am I?" is more of a question today than "Who am I?"

People are pushing down to the deepest realms of their beings. They are searching for a relationship with the universe, for some cause, some root force to grasp. What they find they call the "Old Religion." To understand this desire for roots, the Christian has to look all the way back to the first feelings of man. What is happening around us now comes out of man's awakening past.

3 The Awakening Past

The occult is so much "bunk" says a professor who has observed college fads.

"No, it's all a part of Satan's attempt to confuse people in the last days," explains a pastor.

"I have never heard of such things," exclaims an elderly church member. "It must be some new thing that the young people are doing."

"It's not new at all," says an occult bookstore owner in Chicago. "It comes out of Celtic folklore. It goes back thousands of years."

Simple answers won't explain or dismiss the occult. The present day interest in the mystical, the magical, and the metaphysical is deeply rooted in the earliest thinking of ancient man.

Having gone through the heady scientism of the seventeenth, eighteenth, and nineteenth centuries, modern man is again finding that he is more deeply involved in the cosmos than test tubes and scientific equipment can measure.

The *Whole Earth Catalog* people today speak ecologically about the earth, and they seek again to be a part of nature. Indian religions with a spiritual view of nature are attractive to the young. Youth object to being manipulated by science or corrupted along with the polluted natural resources. They are looking again to the past and to mother earth and to the simple life with nature. To understand modern man's quest for occult powers, we need to understand his desire to be one with nature, respecting it and being part of its total harmonious plan.

Twentieth-century people with a rationalistic frame of

reference have difficulty in understanding the occult interest in spirits, spells, and curses. But these practices come out of nature worship and have affected man and his behavior from the beginning of time.

To understand the history of the occult, we must look beyond the witchcraft of eighteenth-century England. Nor will we understand it if we isolate the events leading to the Toulouse Inquisition of 1335. And it is too simple to see the occult merely as a reaction to the Christian faith, though evidently St. Augustine did when he referred to the witches of the fourth century.

Western man can trace his occult history back to many so-called "starting places." Greece and Rome had their stories of the occult. Horace, the Roman poet, described witches who used bones and herbs and black lambs to summon the dead. Medea is one of the best-known Greek sorceresses. Homer speaks of witchcraft in his writings. Chaldean and Babylonian history reveal occult practices, and the Old Testament tells of the witch of Endor in 1 Samuel 28. But even this doesn't go deep enough to explain the beginnings of the occult.

The occult has taken many historical tangents. Scholars can trace different forms of occult religion historically by way of different avenues and through different philosophies, each altered by the impact of various civilizations. But the real roots of the occult go back farther than recorded history and philosophy. The occult begins practically at the dawn of man's existence.[1]

On the wall of a cave at Ariége, France, there survives a painting called the "Sorcerer" or the "Magician." It is the picture of a man in animal skins wearing horns and walking upright. The drawing is dated by the *Encyclopedia Britannica* as far back as 30,000 B.C. Similar paintings or carvings have been found on rocks and the walls of caves across the European continent from Spain to the

[1] For further information about the history of the occult, see the following books:
Crow, W. B., *A History of Magic, Witchcraft and Occultism*. London: The Aquarian Press, 1968.
Materials Toward a History of Witchcraft, collected by Henry Charles Lea. Vol. 1, edited by Arthur C. Howland. New York: Thomas Yoseloff, 1957.
Parrinder, Geoffrey, *Witchcraft: European and African*. London: Faber and Faber, 1958.
Summers, Montague, *The History of Witchcraft and Demonology*. New York: University Books, Inc., 2nd edition, 1956.
Wilson, Colin, *The Occult*. London: Hodder and Stoughton, 1971.

Soviet Union. Such horned gods were known all over the ancient world.

Rome, Greece, Egypt, and all of the Celtic areas had some form of a horned god. Similar pictures or carvings have been found in Africa, the Islands of the Pacific, and America, among the Eskimos, and even among the North American Indians.

Probably ancient man first associated this figure with hunting. But later it undoubtedly became a symbol of fertility as well. This development seems to have been taken by the Greeks in their goat man with horns known as Pan. This conception is also, most likely, the beginning of the Devil's picture that man still points to as descriptive of Satan.

Fertility worship was basic to the very existence of man. The period between 9,000 and 7,000 b.c. reveals artifacts showing fertility goddesses. These were refined to become the well-known Artemis of Ephesus and Ishtar of Babylonia. There were others, too—Cybele, Demeter, Ceres, Aphrodite, and so forth. All were a part of fertility cults which were sometimes accompanied by sacred prostitution.

But still, the temple goddesses and the fertility rites are more of a branch than the mainstream of the occult. The center of the occult, particularly witchcraft, goes back to the time when man was struggling for existence. No matter how these rituals evolved, even to the modern witch's esbats and sabbats, they were originally tied in with nature worship. Birth and existence, life and death were great mysteries, and these mysteries were basic to ancient religion. From these roots came the witchcraft and astrology with all of their many divisions that we find in the world today. The history of the occult is, in a sense, the history of the earth, the universe, fertility cults, and particularly women.[2]

From earliest times, when roving tribes lived off the land, women were important. The women were left in the camp or the enclosed protected place to take care of domestic duties and to handle the children. Men hunted and took from the land. The women began to discover and use nature.

Women worked with agriculture. At first this may have been only the gathering of herbs and plants. But later, they began to

[2] On the role of women in witchcraft, see Frank Donavan, *Never on a Broomstick* (Harrisburg, Pa.: Stackpole Books, 1971) and Ian Ferguson, *The Philosophy of Witchcraft* (London: George C. Harrap & Co., Ltd., 1924).

cultivate crops and even to raise some animals within the enclosure.

When her children became ill, the woman had to seek the herbs or weeds that she had seen the animals eating. From years of trial and error came her knowledge of what were antidotes and what were poisons.

As the women worked together, preparing food and relieving the pain of illness, they must have talked. Perhaps they philosophized about the powers that seemed to control them. Theirs was a mysterious world, a world very much alive. There were forces all around them—dangerous, baffling forces. They saw the current in the river, the effect of the wind in the trees, the changing face of the moon, and the destructive storms, and they speculated, "Where did the tides come from?" "Why is the sun warm?" "Does the world die in the autumn?"

Woman probably reflected on the hot summer and the winter storms and wondered about human life cycles. Scholars picture her on winter evenings, gathered with her children and other women around the fires, speculating about the meaning of life and death and putting values and explanations on that which she could not understand. Such speculation was the beginning of a primitive, superstitious religion.

Woman had fertility, the mysteries of life within her. Without her there would be no children, no men to hunt and fight. The woman could cultivate the plants, choosing the right soils to make them grow. She understood the seasons and knew when the land would produce again. Later she had the tools, the pitchfork and the broom, and they took their place with her.

Her spells and magic potions brought healing. To her the men came with their cuts and bruises and broken bones, and she soothed the pain with her herbs and wisdom about healing ointments. She knew and used such drugs as belladonna, foxglove, and henbane. She was probably familiar with the properties of the poppy, the nightshade, and Indian hemp.

She recognized the energy in fire and developed the art of cooking, and these, too, became a part of her religious knowledge. Fire could warm, cook, consume, and destroy. Animal parts had different values. The unusual formation of the animal intestines, brains, and bones was material for religious speculation.

Woman's craft became a religion and some women became the

religious practitioners. Woman was, thus, the priestess, prophetess, and, in conjunction with nature, the goddess of fertility and productivity. And it stood to reason that if a woman could bring out a fever by her spells and herbs, and could cure a sick child, then surely her spells and potions could work the opposite way to bring pain and even death. She could instill fear by suggestion or spells. Her magic made her both the ancient physician and the ancient voodoo practitioner.

The life struggle and the basic necessities for existence became the ingredients for the occult religious practices. Fire, herbs, spells, incantations, and fertility—these were the woman's domain. The dark and the mysterious, the stars and the sun, and the influences of nature were the province of the women and formed the roots of witchcraft, astrology, mind science, and satanism.

It would have been foolish for men to have challenged such a power. By her guidance the evils in the night, the spells cast by others, and the demons and the powers of the unseen world could be expelled or appeased. Her potions and magic made people strong, or weaken and die.

Folk beliefs, religious occult rituals, and witchcraft came out of these primitive nature beliefs. Throughout recorded history, witchcraft has been blamed for the destruction of crops, the tearing of fishermen's nets, the spoiling of ale, and has been given as the reason that cows went dry. And whether scholars trace the occult back through the various Greek gods and goddesses, animism, fertility religions, or the many superstitions of the folk beliefs, the roots of the occult in man's past are basically the same.

The Saxons had "wiccas" or wise ones. The Romans and the Normans had their cultic beliefs, as did other peoples. These cults did not end with the coming of the Christian faith. Christians proclaimed deliverance in Christ from fear of the unknown, the coming of God himself to dwell with man, and a freedom to live in peace and harmony with God. But those who did not hear or would not believe still held to their folk cults. These beliefs continued to develop as a part of each culture with accompanying rituals and incantations.

People living in the modern world, with their understanding of science, find it difficult to comprehend the mysteries, the fear of the unknown, and the belief in spells and witchcraft that dominated and controlled people's thinking during the period of the Middle

Ages and before. Stories abound of vampires and dragons and giants, magic powers and potions and charms. Astrologers were consulted by even the well-educated. Man's early religions were carried from generation to generation, changing and developing over the centuries.

During the Middle Ages, the witch, like her ancestors, was not just a religious leader; she was also the medical practitioner. She had power with her spells and medicines. If a housewife or someone else in the village had a need, she went to the woman who was particularly good at conjuring up the right combination of herbs or casting the most powerful spells. When modern cartoonists draw an old hag stirring her caldron over a fire and bringing up a witches' brew, their picture is probably not too farfetched. This person would be the medical practitioner brewing up a special potion for a sick villager. As strange as this conception seems to the modern mind, it was serious business then. Even the professional doctors in the cities had similar practices. For example:

> Queen Anne knighted an oculist whose great work was the discovery that putting a louse in a blind eye tickled it, making the eye moist and "quickening the spirits."
>
> The professional cure for diabetes was a dried and powdered mouse, taken for three consecutive mornings.
>
> The gall of a black puppy was the sure cure for epilepsy.
>
> The powdered bones of human mummies in red wine were used as the cure for dysentery.

As the occult developed out of the old folk beliefs, it evolved into a system of ritual and belief practiced by people as they needed power, an escape, an identity, and a fellowship. Much of this system centered around forms of witchcraft. By the time of the Middle Ages it was well formulated, including acts paralleling and opposing the rituals and practices of the established church.

People in the Middle Ages did not necessarily give up their church going when they became witches. There are many cases on record of people faithful in their church attendance and also in their witchcraft or demon worship. They were able to enjoy the mystical experiences of both rituals, without fully understanding either one.

Those who wanted to be admitted into a witches' group had to promise to devote themselves totally, body and soul, to their devil. These people were not necessarily avowed satanists who realized what they were doing. These were ignorant people. The modern Christian who asks, "How could they do that when they were also members of the church?" must remember that for many being part of the church had little or nothing to do with a commitment to Jesus Christ.

The grand master of a coven was often called "lord," "god," or Lucifer, and the witches paid homage to him with a kiss. In Scotland, witches demonstrated their fidelity to the master by laying one hand on the head, the other on the sole of the foot, and giving everything in between to him.

The witches met at a central place, usually in a woods near a crossroads where people could come together easily. They celebrated at least four special occasions called sabbats: All Hallows' Eve, May Eve or Beltane, St. Thomas Day, and Midsummer's Eve. There were other meetings, too, called esbats. These were weekly business meetings where they exchanged reports of magic works that they had done since the previous meeting and gave one another advice.

After the ritual and feasting and frenzied dancing in a circle, the sabbats usually ended in an orgy. Male witches had sexual intercourse with female witches, or, if the coven was all women, then the devil or grand master had intercourse with any of them. People who witnessed this sexual expression regarded it in different ways. For some it was seen as wanton pleasure. Others viewed it as an expression of freedom for women who had little excitement in their daily lives.

At home, women were chattels. They had no chance for an education, no voice in the affairs of the organized church, and little or no influence with their husbands or masters. But in witchcraft they had power and fun. One story about a young woman may be descriptive of many. She was attractive but married to a rather drab farmer. She was quick, he was dull witted. So when she was accosted by the grand master, she agreed to enjoy the pleasures of witchcraft. For her it was probably an escape from boredom.

There were several styles of witchcraft practiced by the people. There were "white" witches, who wanted to do good things for people, and "black" witches, who wanted to do harm. And then there were the committed satanists.

Some satanists did not think of themselves as Devil owned or even anti-Christian. They were simple people who enjoyed the excitement and power of Devil worship. Others purposely renounced their faith, took a new name, made a pact with Satan, and were baptized in his name. These satanists practiced the black mass.

The black mass incorporated the ritual of the sabbat along with anti-Christian blasphemy. A flat land with a wooded area was chosen for the mass. The woods were the equivalent of the church choir; the flat area was the sanctuary; and the open ground was the nave. There was usually a stone altar erected, with a large black wooden image of Satan in front of it. The body of the image was human; the feet, head, and hands were those of a goat. A torch usually burned between his horns or someplace nearby.

The priestess began the ritual by saying, "Save me, lord Satan, from the treacherous and the violent." Then there was an introit and prayer followed by all of the other ritual acts of the regular mass, changed to fit the worship of Satan. Sometimes a banquet was held. Toward the end of the ceremony the priestess stretched out naked on the stone altar, and her ceremonial work was then taken over by a man who was officially called the devil.

Acknowledging Satan as god, the people recited a creed. Then they practiced the fraction, in which the priest-devil took a toad, instead of the Communion host which the Catholic priest used in the church mass, and symbolically beheaded it, blaspheming the symbolized broken body of Jesus. Other times they would use the actual elements of the church mass, stolen by church attenders and sacrilegiously served on the body of the priestess as she lay on the altar. At the end of the rites, there was a curse pronounced instead of a blessing, and spells were cast on certain animals in the name of Lucifer.

History is full of stories about some of the rituals practiced in the black mass—drowning unbaptized babies, boiling and drinking the blood of slain children from a chalice at the altar, using their intestines in unusual ceremonial acts, and perverted sexual activities. Stories are told of people killing a child, attending the funeral with the parents, and the next night disinterring the body for their use.

The thought of stealing babies and killing them in Satan worship is not totally illogical. When the emphasis that was put on the baptism of a baby by the church is understood, the motive of a committed satanist in killing a baby can also be understood. Since, according to the church, the unbaptized baby could not enter into heaven because of original sin, the killing of an unbaptized baby would postpone the day of judgment by delaying the completion of the proper number of people required for heaven before the destruction of the world. According to this twisted theology, it was to the satanists' advantage to kill babies. In other words, people believed that taking these babies for Satan was a way of holding off the day of judgment.

Historians are hesitant to confirm many of the stories about the various practices in Satan worship. But then no one is absolutely certain that all of the current stories of blood sacrifices and ritualistic murders in Satan worship today are true. Those who believe can find many examples in the newspapers to support their beliefs. Those who do not see such reports as the talk of scared people.

From Berne, Switzerland, there is such a case of satanism reported to have occurred about 1550. A young man was being initiated into the sect of Satan. On the day of initiation he was accompanied to the church by his sponsors and before them he denied Jesus Christ, denied his baptism, denied the church, and paid homage to the Devil. Then he drank a liquor made of fluids boiled from the bodies of children, victims of Satan worshipers. When he drank, it was said that his heart was then ready and able to conceive the images of the various rites of his new religion. Historians write that when he was sentenced to die at the hands of the Inquisitors, he renounced his new religion and "came back to the faith."

Some scholars believe that the black mass was not so much a religious act as it was a form of social protest. They describe these people as the anarchists of their day. They were the rebellious people, reacting against the church. The church represented the state and the oppressive land owners. Satan became the god of the serfs, the god of liberty.

The formalized religion of the church did little to liberate people from their dependency on the occult. The message of deliverance, that might have been preached by the church, became instead a message of pressure and power, causing people, in reaction, to hold more firmly to the occult beliefs that gave them a sense of personal involvement in religion, as well as freedom and pleasure.

The growth of the occult in the Western world parallels the ecclesiastical power and spiritual weakness of the established church. Heresy, superstition, satanism, and the corruption of the church are all historically intermingled. Nonetheless, lines of battle were being drawn between the church and the occult, setting the stage for the Inquisition and witch-hunts. The battle was waged with church power, not with the appeal of the message of Jesus.

There was no bright light of biblical witness by which the dangers of the occult could be distinguished and overcome. The church was not a beacon that could guide men and women out of heretical beliefs, because there were many heretical teachings and practices within the church itself. In its attempt to illuminate the dangers of the occult, the church was at best a flickering light.

4

The Church:
A Flickering Light

Throughout its two thousand years of history the church has been a flickering light. Sometimes the light has been very bright, other times very, very dull. Its reaction to the occult has paralleled its understanding of biblical theology and its own faithfulness to God. When the church has been spiritually strong, it has handled the occult knowledgeably, firmly, and with love. When it has been weak, it has been confused, dogmatic, and cruel.

THE CHURCH'S STRUGGLE WITH THE OCCULT

Persecution of people practicing the occult did not begin with the church. During the time of Octavius, Anthony, and Lepidus, astrologers and charmers were banished from Rome. Books on sorcery were burned. Augustus punished practitioners as people who despised the gods. Wizards were executed, and people trafficking in the occult were exiled by the Roman Senate under Tiberius. The harsh enforcement shows the degree of influence the black arts had on the people during the time of the Caesars.

Enlightened Christians who know something of the Salem witch-hunts sometimes negate or downgrade the influence of witchcraft because of their embarrassment about the way that the church handled it. Many modern Christians have come to believe that the church overreacted to the simple superstitions of an uneducated people. In thinking this way, the well-meaning Christian ignores a fundamental point. Although the church often misunderstood some aspects of the occult and was sometimes just as evil in its own way as the people it tried to suppress, the church was correct in many of its main assumptions and fears about the occult. Although the church reacted with cruelty over the years, the cause for this reaction, the influence and control of Satan, was very real.

If the modern Christian, through embarrassment, wants to ignore or play down or laugh at this historical reaction to the occult, he must not play down the influence of Satan as well.

At first, the preaching of the disciples about Jesus was positive, pulling people away from their nature gods and superstitious fears. The Christian faith grew quickly, spreading throughout the known world. These early Christians taught about a real Satan, a Satan who had driven man from the Garden, led him into sin, brought about his fall, and who tried but failed to overcome Jesus. They preached a Satan who was defeated by the power of the resurrection and, although allowed to be on this earth for a little while, rules only until Jesus comes again.

The church fathers also spoke very clearly about the Devil, particularly about his desire to lead men astray, though they sometimes argued about the degree of Satan's power. Cyprian, Eusebius, Origen, Ambrose, St. Hilary, and Jerome all spoke of the power of Satan and his control over men.

As the church grew in numbers, problems of organization and education began to affect the degree to which it could closely follow the teaching of Jesus and the apostles. The very size of the church, with local churches established in many cities, led to struggles for power and influence. As more and more people came into the church, the leaders found careful teaching more and more difficult. Now Christians found it altogether too easy to carry on some aspects of their earlier cultic practices. In some instances, the church even tried to use the old cultic practices as means of explaining the Christian faith. Hence, saints, shrines, demons, and angels reflected both the biblical background of Christian teaching and the cultic backgrounds of the new Christians.

The Christian message became clouded with dogmas and teachings from many sources. For example, the *Revelation of Paul*, a heretical writing of the fourth century, speaks of guardian angels whose task it is every day to report to God on the activities of particular souls. Angels were assigned to people. Some were helpful, others were demons who deluded or tempted them. There were good angels, there were bad angels, there were demons. These brought illness, misfortune, suffering, and an invitation to sin. Everything in some way or other controlled people. They felt manipulated.

There are many legends from history about the efficacy of the various methods for deliverance from evil. There was a battleground in man, demons on the one hand, God on the other. Satan was thought to enter into treaties or compacts with other human beings so that he could accomplish his evil in the world. Demons could act in human bodies; they could reproduce themselves and create other demonic beings. They possessed the old women who stole children and cooked them. They became the witches and the evil spirits—the men and women of the shadows.

When people were told that they *must* go to church, they *must* follow the Mass, and they *must* keep certain ritualistic practices in a very ironclad, rule-laden formalism, without either spiritual warmth or comprehension, then they began to gravitate to the familiar cults and religions of their forefathers that offered them some pleasure and excitement and power.

People responded to the many church holy days with their own occult holy days. The magic in the church was replaced with the magic of witchcraft. The mass in the church was twisted into the black mass of the woods. The church was austere and oppressive; the night meetings of the witches were free and sensual. The church offered religious laws; it did not offer an exciting, life-changing Christian faith.

There was a constant battle between the church and Satan. Satan was at work in the people satisfying their needs through the various forms of the occult, from mild spells and charms to the black mass. But he was at work in the church, too, corrupting it and blocking the doctrines of God with the dogmas of men. Yet, the church, for all of its weaknesses, still had some perception. Church fathers had enough understanding to know that they were fighting a powerful enemy.

Unfortunately, in its attempt to eliminate the corrupting influence of Satan, the church adopted the methods it had learned from the world. With the legal, economic, and political power of its structure, it sought to wipe out heresy. Instead of winning people to a personal commitment to Christ, and thus overcoming Satan with the new birth, it simply tried to eliminate anyone who taught or practiced anti-Christian heresies. This Inquisition was violent and it swept up people indiscriminately. Anyone who practiced folk religion, witchcraft, sorcery, cast spells, or called into question some of the church doctrines was punished as a heretic.

In the early twelfth century, Tanchelin, also called Tanchelm, an incoherent madman whose rantings drew a certain following, declared his intention to destroy the church. Some historians have written that he encouraged his followers to practice all of the foul devices that man could conceive to do. Evil, even unmentionable, things were practiced to the point where everything good was considered to be bad and must be shunned as an offensive thing.

Some of the accusations against him got out of hand. Tanchelin did disagree with the church's stand on sexual relations, but, like Peter of Bruys and other well-known heretics, he was accused of a lot of things that he didn't teach. The church listed him as the cause of many occult sexual rituals, even though he was more of a wild anarchist than a practicing satanist. It was indicative of the confused state of the church that it could not distinguish between doctrinal heresy and radical behavior. Tanchelin was a heretic in that he opposed the teachings of the church, but no one really bothered to find out where his actual heretical teaching left off and accused heretical teaching began.

People ignored much of the condemnation leveled at the occult by the church. There was little exemplary life-style in the church to follow. Its voice was loud, but its practice was louder. There was magic in the fields and there was magic in the church. If the occult was unchristian, so was much of what went on in the church. A good example was the moral behavior of churchmen. They condemned the behavior of the witches, but the witches knew what the priests were doing. If there were orgies at the crossroads, there were rumored to be orgies in the church as well.

At least two popes were involved in sex scandals. And if such things happened at the higher ecclesiastical levels, they were apt to happen with the parish priests who knew how to convince illiterate country girls that giving them pleasure was a holy thing to do. Thus, when the church loudly condemned people for practicing in the countryside what the church leaders did in their own cloisters, the condemnation was ignored.

The church became alarmed at what was happening to it and around it. It reacted to the radical teachings that were part of the occult, without realizing and correcting its own influence which drove people into the occult. But, reactionary or not, the church did recognize a satanic intervention in these other teachings and practices.

People involved in witchcraft today explain that their rites are really an ancient religion. They believe that when the Christians got into control, they attacked the "Old Religion" just because it was different. There are sophisticated Christians today who feel the same way, not understanding the theological and emotional corruption that the occult plants in the souls of men.

When a Christian who prides himself in being broad-minded looks at the attacks of the church on folk religions, he is aroused and angered. "Why couldn't they let the people have their superstitions? Why couldn't they let them worship their earth goddesses or their horned god? What could be so wrong with a few spells and chants? They are innocent enough!" But nothing that Satan gets into and controls is innocent.

The heresy in the occult, historically and today, is that people try to find their knowledge of God by means other than God's revelation of himself. Historically, people who followed the route of the occult were trying to fill the void in their souls that could only be filled with the Christ of God who came offering full and abundant life.

Modern man who flirts with the occult is doing the same thing. Christians are not concerned about the occultist's sexual dancing, his spells, or his witches' curses and herbs, as such. The Christian is motivated, not by a prudish reaction to another's pleasure but by a burden for the lives and souls of people, to speak out against the occult. Following the human route to God has always been the ruse that Satan has used to control people. He will always give a satisfying counterfeit which causes people to look away from the outstretched love of God offered to the world through Jesus Christ.

The church of the Middle Ages was confused. But as cloudy as the heresy issues were, as corrupt as the church was, and as innocent as some folk practices seemed to be, the church was correct in its alarm. When Innocent VIII issued his Papal Bull on December 5, 1484, calling for witches to be burned at the stake, he was not just disturbed about mild superstition. He was opposing real heresy. The church leaders may have handled the occult in an inhumanly cruel manner, but they did try to handle it.

THE WITCH-HUNTS

The witch-hunts began early. Alexander III in 1163 asked the Council of Tours to act against a resurgence of the old Manichean heresy which came alive some four centuries after it was thought to have been destroyed. The Third Lateran Council in 1179 again looked into this. In 1184, some of the heretics were mentioned by name in a Bull issued from Verona by Lucius III. It was becoming more and more acceptable to seek out and punish heretics.

By 1235, the term "Inquisition" was being freely used. On December 13, 1258, Pope Alexander IV addressed his Papal Bull against witchcraft to the Franciscan Inquisitors. In 1330 a witch was burned in Southern France. Over the next twenty years some six hundred people were sent to the stake for heresy or witchcraft. When the Black Death swept through Europe in the mid-fourteenth century, killing as much as 25 percent of the population, many in the church were convinced that it was God's punishment for the widely practiced witchcraft.

By the fourteenth century, the popes began to respond in even stronger measures to the occult. John XXII in 1318 ordered inquests into a number of people in his court who were accused of magic and other evil crafts. In 1320, he issued firm orders giving Inquisitors the right to act against those who sacrificed to demons or worshiped them in some other way. Gregory XI in 1374 was distressed to learn that some of his clerics invoked demons. In 1437, Eugenius IV deplored the fact that many Christians were sacrificing to demons and paying homage to them. Nicholas V, in 1451, gave Inquisitors specific orders to proceed against diviners.

A group that in the ninth century was tolerated as a few deluded women, who claimed to have ridden around in the sky on brooms, became, by the fifteenth century, Satan's band that had to be hunted down. In 1487, a book entitled *Hammer of Witches* was published by two European witch-hunters. It became the manual for Inquisitors. With the aid of this book they knew exactly how to discover witches. This manual presumed guilt at the outset and prescribed trickery, torture, or whatever else was necessary to pull a confession out of the accused.

Gnostics, as well as witches, became the hunted people. The term "Gnostic" comes from the Greek word, *gnosis*, which means knowledge. The Gnostics claimed to have a knowledge which was hidden from other people. In general, they believed that the world of men, in the flesh, had been created by a Demiurge, often associated with the God of the Old Testament, and that men could not free themselves from this evil bond until they received this secret higher knowledge. Subject to the Demiurge, men could not be held responsible for their evil acts. But as they were initiated into the mysteries of the hidden knowledge, they attained purity of spirit and were fitted to dwell on high.

Over the centuries Gnostic teaching emerged again and again. Many of the attempts to define a pure, spiritual world in distinction from an evil, material world were related to this Gnostic heresy. Gnosticism, with its emphasis on the conflict between good and evil powers, mysteries, and hidden knowledge, was often coupled with witchcraft and satanism.

Gnosticism fitted in with the occult because it had a certain "logic." Believing that man did not have free will, Gnostics taught that he could not by his own nature sin. Therefore, it was God who willed sin and was the source of evil. Since God was the Creator of the world, the world as well as God was evil. Therefore opponents of God, the worshipers of the "higher intelligence," were the good people.

This same philosophy of gnosticism is basic to the occult movement today. Man's essential goodness, the denial of sin and evil, and the "knowledge" of a "real God" by means other than God's revelation of himself are modern doctrines that have come out of ancient gnosticism. The twentieth-century occult revival is rooted in Gnostic heresy.

One particular Gnostic sub-sect mixed with the witchcraft and satanism of the Middle Ages. The "Messalians" taught that Satan was to be honored as divine. They could do this best by projecting outrage and blasphemy on Jesus Christ. Also, by practicing the sins forbidden in Scripture, they showed their defiance to the "evil creator." Witchcraft, satanism, and gnosticism overlapped, and the church sought to eliminate all of them.

Once the desire to find witches excited the Inquisitors, it got out of hand and witch-hunting soon was rampant. By the 1600's professional witch-hunters were being hired by whole towns. They usually found their witches by pricking them with a needle. If there was no pain and no blood, it was then concluded that the accused were witches. But in one particular town when twenty-seven out of thirty women brought forward were found to be witches, this method became suspect. It was found then that the witch-hunters were using retractable instruments with a point that went back into the handle so that there would be no pain or blood when the instrument was placed against the skin.

Witch-hunts were usually conducted in the open and became a public spectacle. So-called witches were stripped, always with a crowd gathered around to watch. The townspeople were pleased to hire the witch-hunters; the hunt made a good show; it instilled fear into people whom they didn't particularly like; and it was good for business.

Witch-hunters made good profits because they always managed to find people who were witches. Their work did not cost the state or town anything, because the expense of the trial was charged to the estate of the person who was condemned or to her relatives. Everybody profited by the witch trials. Crowds were drawn, so the local tavern owner always made extra money. If people came from a distance, the innkeeper made money. Sometimes he even gave a banquet for those who came to the trial. If there was a burning, the woodcutter who made the stake was paid and so were the suppliers of peat or coal. Both the jail keeper and the torturer were paid.

Prices got so out of hand that towns had to set up rates for the various aspects of witch-hunting. Prices were set for torture, listing the fees that could be charged for different types of torture. For example, a town council had to set the highest amount that could be charged for crushing a finger or cutting off a hand. They determined how much an executioner could charge for the rope that he used to tie a person to the stake. If the execution was by quartering, then the rates listed included the cost of the horses as well as transporting the remains of the body.

Witches usually confessed their crimes when the torture got extreme enough. Since the worship of Satan was heresy, and heresy was punishable by death, no one would confess readily. So torture was necessary to force a confession. And when the torture became so severe that death was more welcome than more torture, the person confessed. In many cases, however, the torture did not stop with the confession, because continued torture was necessary to get the witch to implicate other witches. Soon the witch was naming other people just to put an end to her own suffering.

In England, torture was not legally allowed, except by a special act of Parliament. But there were many ways to get around that.

Prison itself was torture because of its filth and cramped conditions. Police investigations were torture. Suspects were hung from the ceiling by their fingers with weights attached to their feet, or they were stretched on the rack, or they had their thumbs and toes crushed in vices.

One of the most popular tests in England and America was swimming the witch. In this test, the right hand was tied to the left foot, and the left hand to the right foot. The person was put into a pond with a rope around the waist. If she floated, she was a witch. If she sank, she was innocent. The reasoning was simple. A witch would not sink because, having denied her baptism, she would be rejected by the water.

There were times when witch-hunters were successfully finding thousands of witches. A person could be accused of witchcraft or Satan worship for any reason at all. When someone was accused, it was practically certain that she would be condemned and burned. Scholars who have researched witchcraft suggest that there are probably several reasons why people continued in witchcraft in spite of the terrible witch-hunts. There was a great pessimism about life. Life didn't offer much in the way of excitement. The church standards for being a Christian were impossibly high. A person could, it was true, be sent to hell for practicing witchcraft, but he could also go to hell for skipping church meetings on Sunday. So if someone, man or woman, was going to be damned, he thought he might just as well be damned for something that was a lot more exciting than skipping mass.

Almost every witchcraft trial was based on circumstantial evidence. People were superstitious. Life was a mystery. People feared what they didn't understand. Illness that couldn't be cured by a doctor was thought to be caused by a witch, and usually the sick person was able to name the witch. If somebody died when a suspicious person was around, then that person was blamed for the death.

The biblical emphasis taught by the Reformation did not put an end to the witch-hunts. The Reformers were just as cruel in their persecution of heretics as the church they left. Protestants and Catholics alike persecuted anyone accused. It was a harsh age.

Anyone could charge a witch, even children. There are cases on record of children accusing their own parents of witchcraft. One little boy confessed that he was carrying on a prank after twenty-two people died by his charges. In England the Reverend George Burroughs was condemned on the testimony of a little orphan girl whom he had befriended. Eighty-five people died in Sweden on the testimony of one eighteen-year-old youth.

In America the Salem witch-hunts are infamous, although not nearly as many people were killed in the colonies as were killed in other countries. Some historians are beginning to find that the colonial courts were far more lenient than legend indicates. For the known twenty-eight deaths for witchcraft in Massachusetts in the seventeenth century, there were hundreds in England, and even larger numbers on the Continent. Nine hundred witches were burned during the witch-hunts in Bamberg, Germany, and five thousand in Alsace. The smaller number in America could be due to the small population in the colonies, or it could be an evidence of the decline in hysteria and fear that was beginning to work itself out about that time.

In England under Elizabeth I, witchcraft was considered treason and was punishable by death. In 1604 this charge was broadened even more to include many anti-church and anti-crown teachings. These laws remained in force until repealed by King George II in 1736. But even the repeal retained a clause condemning witchcraft, sorcery, and enchantment. Queen Victoria had this modified, and in 1951 the laws against witches were repealed.

The witch-hunts were both a religious and cultural problem. Self-preservation, not wickedness, drove people to put witches to death. To blame them for fearing witchcraft is like blaming them for not believing in the germ theory of disease. They really didn't know any better. And if torture was severe, everything was severe at the time.

In spite of their biblical teachings, the Puritans got into the witch-hunts like everybody else. The fear of witches was a community issue, a part of their culture. They simply added their scriptural beliefs to their cultural attitudes. They were wrong in their behavior, but we cannot fault them any more than we can be overly critical of people today who improperly mix their scriptural and cultural beliefs. They read their Bibles with culturally distorted vision and find Scripture to support their already chosen position.

After the witch-hunts ended, there followed a period of evangelistic preaching in America and England. The Wesleys and others brought people back to a biblical faith and a Christian life-style, at least in regard to the cruel treatment of witches. But they still practiced cruelty to their black slaves.

Between the biblical emphasis on the value of man and the improved knowledge of medicine and psychology, there was ushered in a quiet period when emotionalism and fear were brought under control. The occult went underground. Those who practiced the black arts and the ancient folk religions did so quietly. Christians who spoke of the power of Satan in men's lives were thought to be a little odd.

With the rising influence of humanism, rationalism, and scientism, the work of Satan was explained away. For almost three hundred years, the occult was a joke to be laughed at by the many when they heard about the bizarre behavior of a few. Then, in the middle of this century, once again the occult began to rise. Today the ancient crafts are rapidly spreading again.

5 The Spreading Craft

"But it's so confusing," says a Christian looking at the burgeoning occult movement. For almost three hundred years the occult seems to have been dormant, and now all around us people are experimenting with clairvoyance and clairaudience, using the tarot cards, worshiping Satan, and casting spells. To the average Christian, all of this is very confusing.

One of the main reasons for the confusion is the intermingling of the various occult practices. In some way or other, they all overlap. There doesn't seem to be a clear distinction between the beliefs of one type of occult practitioner and the beliefs of another. "Where does one end and another begin?" asks the bewildered Christian. "I don't understand it."

"Of course you don't understand it," explains a dedicated Science of Mind church worker. "You take a little bit from this teaching and a little bit from that teaching and you put it all together. Nobody has the whole truth."

The modern occult movement is a do-it-yourself religion. Borrowing freely from one another, there are spiritualists who believe in reincarnation and spiritualists who don't. There are witches who practice clairvoyance and witches who don't. Some mediums are involved also in astrology, others are not. In their searching for an understanding of the powers around them and an experience with other dimensions, they gravitate to whatever seems to appeal to them. In his attempt to understand the forces of the cosmos and his place in the overall pattern, the occult believer is always looking for some new way to expand his consciousness.

The religions of the occult, whether they include the study of horoscopes or the worship of Satan, are built on man's quest for completion and fulfillment. The answers in the occult come not from Divine revelation but from human speculation.

Any listing of occult subjects may range from forty-five to more than one hundred different areas of involvement. Since the different occult beliefs can overlap at any point, depending on the people who practice them, categories have to be separated arbitrarily. However, there are some basic differences between the various forms of the occult. An understanding of these forms can help the Christian be alert and responsive to the occult as it spreads around him.

ASTRAL PROJECTION

To discover that you can leave your body, travel to other areas and other times, and be free of physical confinements while moving as a spirit is an exciting experience. Some people claim to have done this by themselves, but usually they seek to do it under the direction of an experienced person who can bring them back into their bodies if they start to drift away. While traveling in their astral bodies, they believe that they can even be transported back into a previous incarnation.

In a Detroit meeting, five people were allegedly moved out of their bodies at the same time. One began singing in Chinese, and the audience was told that she was doing an ancient Chinese hand-dance that she had learned in a previous incarnation. Others claimed to be transported back to experiences as American Indians. The crowd was fascinated.

People who experience this travel outside their bodies not only are aware of what they are doing, but also describe things that they discovered in their travels. They are left with a sense that they can move out of their bodies at will, that their bodies do not control them, and that they are not limited to time and space. The experience is very liberating; they are explorers of a spiritual dimension.

One fear is always present among those who engage in astral travel. They worry about being left outside of their bodies. Leaders caution people to tell them if they feel that they have not yet returned.

Astral projection is based on a theory of motion. Something

moving always moves something else. Even the wave of a hand moves the air around the hand which in turn moves something else. The same expanding effect is seen by throwing a pebble into a pool. Leaders in astral projection claim that they can send motion out or draw it in by the use of their hands. Thus by the motion of their hands they can pull the astral body out of the physical body. Although leaders deny that they are using hypnotism, the rhythmic movement of their hands is very hypnotic. When the subject is in a trance state, he is told what "incarnation" he is returning to.

In one particular meeting a subject was told that her hands would rise involuntarily. "Oh, no, they won't," she said as she tightly clasped her hands. The leader tried by suggestion and hypnotic movement to get her hands to rise, but they didn't. After trying again and again, he finally turned to the audience and announced with great satisfaction, "You see, this proves that you cannot force a person to do what he does not want to do." He then launched into a reassuring speech about being safe in your body unless you want to leave. No one can force another to leave his physical body or take him into astral travel against his will.

The audience was satisfied with this explanation of his failure. He then successfully got others to raise their hands and the audience was ecstatic. He then tried another experiment.

He tried to make five people picture the same scene in their minds. By suggestion he encouraged the people until they were all seeing the same Indian on horseback, on the same hill next to the same pine tree. But one man didn't stop there. He went on to describe things in his mind picture that the leader hadn't suggested. Obviously he was taking a different trip to a different place. When the leader couldn't get the man to "see" only what the others were seeing in the location where they were traveling, he finally exclaimed with excitement, "He's farther back; he's got a larger view."

During the entire three-hour evening, whatever he did was pronounced a success. The several hundred people, mostly young because the meeting was advertised as a teenagers' night, left with a thrilling sense of awe at the power of astral projection. Many signed up for further exposure through a group that was forming.

ASTROLOGY

With elaborate charts the life of a person can be drawn and studied astrologically. Hundreds of thousands of people will not start their day without first studying their horoscopes. The believer in astrology is convinced that he is functioning in conjunction with the planets and stars. Indeed, the entire order of the universe guides his life.

There is a cosmic interrelatedness in the universe. The sun, moon, and stars all seem to have an influence on each other and the earth. We, too, are in balance with nature, say the believers in astrology. If this is so, to understand ourselves, we have to understand our relationship to these forces. We are influenced by the planets and the stars just as the tide is influenced by the moon.

Astrologers claim that the universe is alive and man is a part of it. He fits into the cosmic whole. Man can understand himself when he understands his personal integration with everything that is happening around him.

This cosmic wholeness is the broad principle that governs the teachings of the *Whole Earth Catalog* people and the new *Place* people. Believers in Yoga see in the coming together of the whole a kind of symphony of being. The sense of wholeness is the principle of fluidity made possible by their body concentration. This wholeness or harmony is one of the reasons that the young are so fascinated by the life-style and religious beliefs of the American Indian. The Indian did not own or manipulate nature, but tried to work and live with it. Organic farming, practiced in many farming communes, is based on a desire to be at one with the earth. Harmony, not opposition or destruction, is attractive.

Astrology also gives man a way of looking at other people. Astrology teaches that all of us fit into the cosmic relationship. I am in relationship, and you are in relationship, and we interact with one another. You do what you do because of your relationship to the cosmos, and so do I. I cannot pass judgment on you because you are fulfilling your pattern. I can, however, try to understand through astrology why you do what you do. In this way I can, perhaps, help you and maybe move in relationship with you as together we fit into the whole structure around us.

Astrology charts have an outer ring showing the signs of the zodiac at the time of birth and an inner chart, divided like a pie into twelve "house cusps," depicting different aspects of earthly life.

The zodiac signs and the planets on the chart affect the houses beneath them. Planets affect each other in different ways. If they are within ten degrees of each other, they are in "conjunction," which causes them to have a strong effect on each other. "Trine" means that they are 120 degrees apart, strongly reinforcing each other, but not as strongly as when they are "sextile," or sixty degrees apart. If they are "square," or ninety degrees apart, there is an obstacle in the way; and real disaster is in the making if they are in "opposition," or a full 180 degrees apart.

By his chart, the astrologer feels that he can see where his strengths and weaknesses are. His good days and bad days fall into a pattern so that by understanding his horoscope, he can understand his life. Astrology gives him a sense of peace and confidence.

"But isn't it simply self-suggestion?" asks a skeptic. "After all, if you know that today is going to be a good day, you move into it with confidence and make it good. If you think that it will be a bad day, it probably will be."

"True," says the astrologer, "but not for that reason. By knowing in advance what is in store for you, you work to eliminate the bad experiences and move in harmony to enhance the anticipated good experiences. Astrology is a strengthening knowledge."

Critics often point to the many wrong predictions by astrologers as proof of fraud. Newspapers have mixed up the dates on horoscopes and printed them anyway, not caring that Saturday's horoscope was really last Wednesday's. More than one self-styled "astrologer" has made a good profit by advertising a personalized horoscope only to send the same mimeographed chart to everyone who sends his dollar! Even two sincere and honest astrologers may predict two entirely different courses for the same person on the same day with the same birth sign.

This discrepancy doesn't bother the believers in horoscopes. They believe that a chart is not just something put out for people to use indiscriminately. It is too personal for that. The chart must center on the whole life of an individual. Astrology is a careful study of a person in relationship to the cosmic forces. He is not like anybody else. So, say the astrologers, it is conceivable that two people under the same sign can have two different astrological charts, and both charts can be correct.

If a horoscope contributes to a person's welfare, his growth and development, then it is considered to be a good chart. According to people who follow their horoscopes, a good astrologer is concerned for his client. He doesn't just give information; he helps to build a person through his relationship with the universal order. He helps to move his client into a contact with the total cosmos, which is a lot different than passing out charts like pills.

Christians need to understand how very religious astrology is to people. It is not a joke or an interesting speculation. People guide their lives by it, and they think of astrology as a type of revelation from God.

Horoscopes fit a life and come out of a whole understanding of the person and the cosmos. In a sense, this "living" chart helps the person to understand his divine purpose and place in the universal order. That's why the birth chart of an individual is considered to be so very important.

To the serious astrologer, man is a part of the essence of God. He is immortal in the sense that he is part of the "God self" and fits into a specific part of the pattern or structure of the universe. To the astrologer's way of thinking, God has done something unique in his birth. He has made him a very real part of the totality of everything.

In the astrologer's understanding the birth chart is very important to God as well. With everything cosmically in order, God impresses upon the newborn child his plan, fitting him into his universal pattern. Using biblical terminology, the astrologer teaches that when a child is born, the position of the sun is the "Son of God," who is at that moment the center of that child's self. God then stays with the child as "comforter" which to the astrologer is the Holy Spirit, or the "Spirit of Understanding." The Holy Spirit helps a child develop by planting in him seeds of intelligence.

The attitude of a follower of astrology toward horoscopes is like the attitude of a Christian to discipleship. He wants to be one with God; he wants to fulfill his responsibilities and consciously be part of the universal purpose or plan. So he seeks cosmic harmony, adjusting his life by his chart. Under God, he feels that he has great potential and can become what he was intended by God to be if he remains loyal to the directions given to him by his chart. By being faithful to his chart, he will not be buffeted by natural or world events and will live harmoniously with God and the universe.

Astrology has captured the interest of many Christians who think that they are following their Lord more exactly. Arguing will not convince them otherwise. A careful biblical explanation of the true meaning of the Lordship of Christ and a loving but firm sharing of the statements of God (Deuteronomy 17:1-5) undergirded by prayer can help a person in astrology begin to see how faithful discipleship and astrology are really in opposition to one another.

AUTOMATIC HANDWRITING

Many believe that messages can come from "the other side" by automatic handwriting. Believers in automatic handwriting think that when a medium contacts the spirit world, his hand can move by impulse to write down the words that the contact person wants to relay to the interested person in this world. The "person" or spirit that moves the medium's hand is known as a "familiar."

As the medium goes into a trance, he seeks to contact his "familiar" on "the other side." Then he asks him questions prepared by the person who is paying to have this contact made. The "familiar" is expected to answer the question either directly with quotes from the departed spirit or indirectly with words about him.

People who go to mediums usually are distressed about someone who died before he could finish some task, or they are in need of particular information from the dead. As the answers come through, the medium writes them down. The words are simple, never elaborate sentences. Usually the medium will ask his client, "Does this have meaning to you?" Usually the words are general enough that they have meaning by association. The eager recipient can generally make sense out of what is written.

People get messages about the past, the present, and the future. Once a person has a successful contact with the spirit world, he will return again and again to his medium, looking for more answers to guide his life.

Answers that come from "the other side" are often helpful. People do seem to get good messages by automatic handwriting. The question to be asked by the alert Christian about automatic handwriting is not "Can it really happen?" but, "Where do the messages come from?" "What is the real source?"

BLACK AND WHITE MAGIC

Black magic is meant to bring harm to someone; white magic is called "good magic."

Magic is as old as man. People familiar with the voodoo dolls of primitive peoples are usually surprised to learn that the ancient Greeks and Romans practiced magic, too. Latin tablets from Carthage record the practice of magic. Charms, spells, incantations supplemented by human fingernail parings, and hair and skin fashioned into the form of a person are all ingredients for magic.

People attempt to win a lover or kill an enemy by casting spells. Although some skeptics think that magic is done strictly by the power of suggestion, they are ignoring the possibility of available forces that come from beyond themselves.

In black magic, the witch concentrates all of his energy on a certain desire while acting out his wish. To kill or injure a person, he may stick a pin into a doll fashioned with something from his enemy's body or house. Or he may paste the person's picture on the wall and throw a knife at it or shoot at it. Driving a nail into an enemy's footprint allegedly can make him lame.

Always the action being carried out is accompanied by specific spells and curses. This combination is believed to send the harmful power out from himself to the person whom he wants to hurt. Many people have been successful enough at black magic to make them firmly believe in its power. Many others, seeing the power at the disposal of black witches, are attracted to it.

Black witches know that their power comes from Satan. But to them Satan is not to be feared but respected as a god. He does not hurt them; rather he gives them what they want. And they like it.

White magicians cast good spells, or so they say. They are afraid of black witches and feel that if they tried to cast black spells, the bad effects would come back at them. Also, conversations with white witches reveal that they have a real concern, even love, for people. Believers in magic say, "Since witches usually get what they want, white witches are good people to know."

White magic uses the same basic spells, charms, and incantations as black magic, but for different reasons. These methods help a man get a promotion by concentrating a spell on his boss, or will help a girl win the boy she wants. They can help a mother determine the sex of her unborn baby or even cause the childless woman to become pregnant. White magic can help a high school team win a football game and a graduating senior avoid the draft.

White witches are offended at the charge that they, too, may be drawing on Satan's power, just as the black witches do. They believe that what they are doing is good for people. They try to keep evil thoughts or perverted ideas from their minds. They honestly try to live and work on a high moral plane. But most of them will admit that the line between white and black magic is very thin.

The witch who could do "good" could also do evil. The witch alone decides what is good and what is evil; the spells for both are quite the same. To cast a spell for healing is considered to be a good thing. But when the sick or injured person says he got that way because of somebody else, the witch is strongly tempted to "get back" at the person who is the cause of an injury, or curse someone who is making his friend's life miserable. Where good ends and evil begins depends completely on the decision of the witch.

In *Today's Witches*, Susy Smith said that it would be good if white witchcraft spread, but she concluded that there is a better chance that black witchcraft will flourish.[1]

THE BLACK MASS

Extreme satanic worshipers, who have committed their lives and souls to the Devil, practice the black mass. The ritual is a reverse of the Roman Catholic Mass, with adoration given not to God, but to Satan. If wine and bread are used, they are purposely desecrated. The altar is usually a young woman, stretched out nude, with the elements served on her body. The final act of "worship" may involve the priest having sexual intercourse with her.

Blood sacrifices are not a required part of the black mass, but ex-satanists tell of drinking the blood of a dog or chicken (sometimes mixed with LSD) and/or eating human flesh, such as a finger chopped off in consecration to Satan. Apparently a missing finger is a religious status symbol for a committed satanist.

The August 16, 1971, issue of *Newsweek* reported that the Los Angeles police were investigating the death of an Orange County schoolteacher "whose heart, lungs and other parts of her body found missing from the grave were used in a bloody sacrifice to the devil."

[1] Susy Smith, *Today's Witches* (Englewood Cliffs, N.J.: Prentice-Hall, Inc., 1970), p. 178.

Anton LaVey, the "Black Pope," denies that there is a black mass performed by satanists, except as a type of psychodrama. In his book *The Satanic Bible,* LaVey says that all Christian worship is a type of black mass because it is a perversion of the original pagan rituals. Since satanists in their worship claim to be going back to "original" forms of worship, they assert that they are not perverting true worship, but the Christians are. The black mass, according to LaVey, is what Christians do every Sunday morning.[2]

CLAIRAUDIENCE AND CLAIRVOYANCE

Clairaudience is "clear hearing"; clairvoyance is "clear seeing." Both are part of the parapsychology "family." They are related to ESP, telepathy, and similar phenomena.

People claiming the gift of clairaudience say that they can hear things at a distance or even before they are said. Clairvoyants describe seeing things at a distance or perceiving events before other people do. There are many documented accounts of people waking up in the night because they have "seen" a loved one in an accident in some other part of the country. Others have known what someone else is going to say before he says it.

There have been many attempts made to discount these psychic abilities. Some say it is all based on unusual guesswork. After all, no one has kept a record of the number of times these people didn't hear or see correctly. But too many experiments have been made, exceeding computerized averages, to deny that some people have a very high degree of clairaudient and clairvoyant accuracy.

The Christian must understand that these powers cannot be lightly dismissed. There are greater dimensions to man and to the world around us than we know or can measure. The mind of man is still an untapped resource. It is very important for the Christian to know that his mind is yielded to the Lordship of Christ. God designed us intricately and with abilities that we may never fully understand. These are abilities that Satan would like to control.

DIVINATION

From the days of the divining rod by which people found water or minerals in the earth, men have been aware of this type of precognition. Divination, whether by a hazel twig to find water or a pendulum to find oil, is a real power. There are stories in

[2] Anton LaVey, *The Satanic Bible* (New York: Avon Book Div., 1969), p. 101.

circulation of diviners finding lost valuables and aiding the police in finding concealed weapons or stolen goods.

Is it just an involuntary muscular movement that makes the rod or pendulum move? If so, why the high rate of accuracy? Divination seems to be a clairvoyant power that some people have developed to a high degree. As in clairvoyance, the question is not "Can it happen?" but, "Who owns the person with the divining gift?" Christians need to be especially certain that any unusual ability they have is included in their surrender of "heart, soul, mind, and strength" to Jesus Christ.

ESP

Extrasensory perception is the ability to perceive beyond the capabilities of the ordinary senses. Many of the human cognitive abilities, such as telepathy, clairvoyance, clairaudience, and kinetic movement, are attributable to ESP.

ESP deals with a psychic factor called "psi." "Psi" involves two factors, mental and kinetic movement. The kinetic aspect known as "PK" or "psychokinesis" is the ability to move or influence an object without touching it or using any kind of measurable or known energy.

The mental aspect of "psi" takes place in telepathy when a kind of thought transfer takes place. Duke University has been actively involved in psychical research into this kind of "psi."

Although tests have repeatedly shown an unexplainable "psi" power, standardized tests in mental and kinetic "psi" have not worked the same way each time they have been tried. Scientifically, an experiment should be repeatable over and over again with the same results. This has not happened with "psi" tests. For example: in tests where someone "guesses" what cards someone else has selected or "wills" certain dice combinations, the success scores have been much higher than a computer predicts they should be. But no standard tests have been devised to cause the same score on the same test in a way that can be repeated over and over again.

Dr. Helmut Schmidt, Director of the Institute for Parapsychology in Durham, North Carolina, said in a *Toledo Blade* news story, April 2, 1972, "We have proved ESP exists. But we don't have the slightest idea how it works. We can't understand it. Nobody at present has a good theory of ESP."

Christians who write off ESP as nonsense have a narrow view of man. It is as foolish to deny ESP as it is to deny radio waves or light rays or radar or anything else beyond what we can know with our immediate senses. Christians need to admit the possible validity of powers like ESP and then find ways to work with people who, in seeking mind expansion, turn away from God into themselves and confusion.

I CHING

I Ching (pronounced ee-ching) is a way of trying to interpret universal laws by understanding the laws of change. *I Ching* promises to help a person make the best of his life by helping him to understand the ebb and flow of change within the universe.

Although many Eastern religions use *I Ching*, it is a cult, rather than a religion, because of its use of divination. It is much older than Taoism and Confucianism, reaching back to the time of King Wen, about 1150 B.C.

Working with predictable cycles of events, *I Ching* attempts to enable man to understand his future. This procedure is not magic or some form of precognition as much as calculation. By knowing the cycles of the universal order, man can identify the trends and know what is coming in his life.

To understand *I Ching*, it is necessary to have an awareness of the Chinese *Yin-Yang* theory or principle. *Yang* is active, strong, male, heaven, and light. *Yin* is passive, female, yielding, weak, birth, and negative. According to the *Yin-Yang* principle the difference between everything in the universe depends largely on how these opposites interblend.

In a manner similar to the *Yin-Yang* theory, the *Book of Change*, or *I Ching*, working on sixty-four hexagrams or constituent processes, has a path or stages. These stages provide 4,096 possible answers to man about how to come into harmony with the universal order.

When a person is ready to inquire of *I Ching*, he takes the *Book of Change* down from its resting place which is clean and always higher than his own shoulders. Then he takes his fifty divining sticks, or six coins, depending on which he chooses to use, and through the ritual of moving the coins or the sticks eventually comes up with a number of sticks (or coins) that lie separate from the others. That is, the sticks end up in one or two trays, or the coins, having been shaken in the hand, fall simultaneously. The number of sticks in one tray or the lie of the coins reveals the response to his inquiry.

The response is interpreted by the text and commentaries of the *Book of Change*. Much of it is based on intuition. But advocates of *I Ching* do not consider intuition a strange or supernormal activity but a sense or power that has to be cultivated and improved, like a skill. By interpreting the response of the sticks or coins, a person can then know what he must or must not do. Thus he gets help in understanding events around him and direction for his life. *I Ching*, operating by the laws of the universe, claims to bring man into harmony with the universe.

The aim of *I Ching* is to help a person become a superior man. A superior man is one who lives in harmony with the laws of the earth, avoids trouble, is able to overcome his own weaknesses, and is one with the supreme wisdom and virtue.

KINETIC MOVEMENT

Kinesis, either telekinesis or some other form of kinetic movement, is the ability to move objects without touching them. Usually it is done by the will of the mind.

Some of the early American psychic activity was based on kinesis. People were able to lift tables, cause rappings in some other part of the house, or break an object from a distance.

Kinetic movement of an object has been substantiated by tests in some cases. It is an awesome power for people to have at their disposal. Those who dabble in it open themselves up to a dangerous demonic manipulation.

MATERIALIZATION

Some people have described ghostlike materializations which have appeared when a spirit has projected itself from the body of a medium or when Satan has been conjured up through spells and incantations. So many people have had experiences of this sort that it is difficult to insist that these phenomena are somehow the products of self-hypnosis.

Spirits seem to materialize through a greyish substance called ectoplasm that usually eminates from the mouth and nostrils of the medium. Mediums have even been photographed with this "soul stuff" coming out of their mouths. In other instances, people have felt that spirits have demonstrated their presence by sound. Pulses come from the spirit world through the medium, it is believed, and then go out to the hearers through a trumpet.

Spirits come when they are called and manifest themselves materially because, according to the mediums, "they obey the will of God." In this context the will of God is explained vaguely as the general law of the universe.

The materialization of spirits is explained on the principle of the conservation of energy. If all energy is conserved, that is, it always exists in some form or other, then it logically follows that "soul" matter continues, whether in this world in a body or spiritually on "the other side." Souls can dematerialize and then rematerialize again. This process is called "Apport," in which an object dissolves, moves to some other place, and materializes again. Because spirits on "the other side" are not in the same form or on the same frequency as the spirits in bodies here, they must show themselves as ectoplasm or speak through trumpets.

Edward Cope Wood, who has written on the spirit world, teaches that materialization explains the resurrection of Jesus. Jesus dematerialized in the tomb, then rematerialized to meet the disciples.[3]

MEDIUMS

Mediums are psychics who claim to hear from departed spirits on "the other side." These mediums are the channels through whom concerned people can receive information about departed loved ones.

Mediums explain that they can "hear" the voice of someone on "the other side" because people in the spirit world are alive, but on a different plane or level. Those in the spirit world can speak by a sort of frequency change through the medium's "familiar or interpreter." It is said that spirits are eager to contact people over here, especially when they first arrive on "the other side," because they are concerned for their loved ones left behind.

Spirits can be contacted on the other side for many years, depending on how long they stay before their next incarnation. According to medium Arthur Ford (that is, according to Ruth Montgomery who contacted Ford on "the other side"), John F. Kennedy cannot be contacted now because he is already back on earth working for peace in the Middle East.

[3] See Edward Cope Wood, *A Personal Testimony to Life After Death* (Philadelphia: Dorrance & Company, Inc., 1963), p. 36.

A powerful medium gathers around himself a loyal clientele who will pay to hear what he learns from the departed spirits. This practice does not mean that a medium is a fraud, although over the years there have been mediums who were frauds. In fact, one fraudulent event is credited with the start of the modern spiritist movement in America.

One night in March, 1848, near Wayne, New York, Katie and Margaretta Fox perpetrated a hoax on their parents that soon had everyone believing that they had a special gift for contacting the spirit world. The two girls, ages twelve and fifteen, were able to get "tapping" responses to their knocking on the wainscoting of their bedroom. They claimed the tapping was a code from the spirit world and that they could get answers to questions by means of the tapping. Their fame spread, and in succeeding years they were acclaimed as great mediums. Katie died in 1892, and Margaretta in 1893, both of chronic alcoholism. Before they died, they confessed that the tapping code from the spirit world was a simple trick done by cracking their toes.

Many mediums, however, are sincere people. Several have been clergymen. They deny that they have anything to do with witchcraft or evil. Yet they admit that there are "evil spirits." They assume that since the spirits they contact advise, guide, and generally help people, they are good spirits and it is beneficial to contact them.

If people say that they are receiving messages from the spirit world, they probably are. But a question worth asking is, "Why can't mediums find anyone on 'the other side' who has met Jesus?" So far, no one claims to have succeeded in doing so.

NUMEROLOGY

In the science of numerology, a person's name means something. Every letter in a name has a numerical equivalent which is influenced astrologically. This concept is an old idea, taken from the Hebrew, in which each letter in the alphabet has a numerical equivalent. Numerologists have taken this concept a step farther, tying it in with reincarnation and astrology to form a religious framework.

Every letter has a corresponding number. For example: A, I, Q, J, and Y are each equivalent to number one; K and R are each equivalent to two; C, G, L, and S are each equivalent to three; D, M, and T are symbolized by four; E, H, and N are each symbolized by five; and on through to the end of the alphabet. A believer in numerology can find the symbolic meaning of his name by adding the numbers in his name. If the total that is derived has two or more digits, these are added together to obtain a single number. The only exceptions are eleven and twenty-two, which have special meanings. The final number, after the adding, is the number that explains the symbolic meaning of a name. Whole volumes have been written about the various explanations of these numerical symbols.

For the numerologist a name, and its numerical equivalent, is a part of a person's birth chart which fits into God's prescribed plan for his life. His birth at a certain time with a certain family and name insures his proper astrological sequence and enables him to work out his karmic pattern.

Many numerologists insist that parents have nothing to do with the time of a child's birth or the name he is given. The soul or spirit, ready for his next incarnation, knows what is lacking in his development and where he can get the lessons that he needs. For example, in his last incarnation he may have been a very selfish individual. Obviously this characteristic is something that has to be changed if he is going to grow toward God and be like God. So he needs to be born into a family that is unselfish and can teach him how to be unselfish. Also, since the whole reincarnation process has to fit into the cosmic whole, he must be born at a specific time so that astrologically he is in harmony with the cosmos. As the cosmos moves, he must move with it, developing and growing into a closer harmony with the universal mind, which to him is God. Finally, he must pick a name that symbolically fits into the whole pattern that is designed for his progressive growth.

So this spirit looks for an unselfish family, picks the date of his birth to fit the right astrological pattern, and chooses a name that numerically has the equivalents that he needs.

What happens when a baby dies at birth or shortly thereafter? Numerologists and reincarnationists explain that the soul/spirit either made a mistake and is going to try again, or God is testing the parents who, of course, are also working out their own particular karmic pattern, improving themselves in this incarnation. "Maybe God is trying to teach the parents some kind of lesson that they haven't yet learned," said a numerologist.

"And what about abortion?" someone asks.

"Oh, no!" says the numerologist, "that would interfere with the whole cosmic plan."

OUIJA BOARDS

Like automatic writing, or kinetic movements, the Ouija board works by the vibrations of the hand, spelling out letters. It supposedly answers people's questions, giving them the guidance that they need for the direction of their lives. For many people this is not a game, it is a serious business and they heed it as seriously as others follow fortune-telling and horoscopes.

The Ouija board concept is based on the "fixed fate" philosophy of an unchanging future. Because God knows the future (he is already there), precognition is possible. Ouija boards, like crystal balls, palm reading, or visions, presume a direct prophetic understanding of what God already knows.

Christians, who reject much of the occult, will sometimes play with Ouija boards. To them it is a game. Those who do should recognize that God has already condemned such practices. Any attempt to find "answers" through a tool that Satan can control is called an abomination by God (Deuteronomy 18:9-14). God wants to guide believers' lives. He reaches out to man through his Son and through the Holy Spirit to do so. Those who ignore him and seek other means reject out of hand the statement of Jesus: "I am the light of the world; he who follows me will not walk in darkness, but will have the light of life" (John 8:12).

PALMISTRY

Palm reading, like card laying and crystal-ball gazing, is a form of fortune-telling. A reader attempts to figure out a person's past and his future by the lines in his hand. More often than not, the reader is right.

There are four main lines on a palm, each given a different meaning. There are also seven sections, divided astrologically by planets, each given a different significance. According to palmistry the way the lines run on her hand shows the number of children a woman has had, or will have. The way a man opens his fist and extends his hand explains the kind of person he is.

More than one Christian, worried about a problem and not finding any answers through prayer, has visited a palm reader "just this one time." In so doing he opens himself up to suggestions and possible demonic control that can influence him far more than he thinks.

PARAPSYCHOLOGY

Parapsychology is a study that goes beyond or alongside the psychology of man. It involves many of the psychic phenomena that are part of the occult practices. Telepathy, clairvoyance, and telekinetic movement are all part of the ESP activities that are studied in parapsychology.

When Apollo 14 Astronaut Edgar Mitchell was in space, he conducted several experiments in parapsychology in conjunction with his ground command center. In so doing he joined an increasing number of American scientists who have been conducting similar experiments since the founding of the American Society of Psychic Research in 1884.

Russian parapsychologists are seeking ways to apply ESP and other "psi" factors scientifically. They hope to develop the human potential in hearing, seeing, knowing, and moving objects by mental energy. They call it "bio-information." The energy involved in all of this is called "bioplasma," which to them is a fourth state of matter.

Bioplasma is always interacting with other matter, and it is this that they see as the aura around something. It is the magnetic force or the vibrations that make possible "skin vision."

Parapsychology is influencing many areas of science. One is in the area of mental health. For example, the Russians and the Americans are asking some serious parapsychological questions: Is a schizophrenic really schizophrenic, or does he somehow pick up the actual thoughts of somebody else? In other words, is he reacting as some other person reacts? Is a person mentally ill if he has this kind of sensitivity?

Is there precognitive sensory perception? Is a person mentally ill when he has visions or dreams or beliefs or is convinced of something when it has not happened? Or does he in fact know something that has *not yet* happened?

Stories told by J. B. Rhine in his book *New World of the Mind* include that of a woman who "saw" her soldier son die in a plane crash. Her screams and hysteria were quite normal for a woman who had actually witnessed such a tragedy, but there was no evidence that her son had in fact died in a plane crash. After the second occurrence of this vision, she was put in the mental wing of a hospital. Doctors saw her as irrational and perhaps mentally ill. It was only after the telegram came with the news that her son had indeed died just exactly the way she had "seen" it, that her doctors realized that her behavior was not unusual under the circumstances.[4]

Parapsychologists are asking many questions. How many people are in mental hospitals because they have had visions or dreams about events that have happened elsewhere or have not yet happened? Does the personality have some extra-physical aspect to it? Can a mind affect the physical just as the physical affects the physical? Can one mind affect another mind?

How does an individual's personality fit into the whole cosmic order? Are we over-against the universal structure? That is, can we function by something more all encompassing than the physical laws?

What about the forces around us, the effects of gravity, the influence of temperature? These are measurable factors. Can they have an effect that is greater than that which can be measured?

What are the limits to the soul of man?

Christians need to be alert to the kinds of questions that are asked in parapsychology. They are basically the same questions that are being asked by the seekers in the occult. Commitment to Christ does not put a Christian in opposition to these questions but gives him a deeper, more encompassing answer.

REINCARNATION

"Reincarnation is necessary because God always was and will be," explains Henry Rucker, a clairvoyant and medium who is Director of the Psychic Research Foundation in Chicago. "Eternal life is promised to us all," he adds. "There is no punishment."

Biblical perfection is possible through reincarnation, according to followers of this occult belief. To them, man has always been and returns to this world over and over again to improve himself. Someday, they suggest, man will be perfect enough to be one with

---

[4] Joseph B. Rhine, *New World of the Mind* (William Sloane Associates, 1968), p. 105.

God. But it is hard to find anybody who knows when that will be. They are always striving, never arriving.

One point is heavily emphasized by reincarnationists: "Do not worry about your life, or wrongdoings or 'sin,' this is not the end of your life." They stress that there is plenty of time in succeeding incarnations for self-improvement. There is no end or judgment; man has many opportunities to improve himself and become like God.

Eternity and the present are together. In other words, we are all living in eternity now. Since there is no separation between time and space and matter, man continues to go right on "over there" from where he left off here. Then he gets ready to return in his next incarnation. Based on the law of karma, reincarnation teaches that man can be born again many times to work out the sins of the past life.

"We choose when to come back as another human being," one witch told a reporter. She said she may be back in three hundred years when the Age of Aquarius has fully arrived.

Being religious, some reincarnationists back up their beliefs with the teachings of Jesus. Jesus said, ". . . I go to prepare a place for you" (John 14:2). Obviously, they say, this means that there is work to be done and progress to be made in the other world. There is a place prepared there for us to improve ourselves and get ready for the next incarnation.

Some believers in reincarnation even teach that there are special missionary "angels of light" who work among spirits to improve their condition for the next incarnation. So, we may even pray for the atheist, and God's missionary angels will come in answer to that prayer to work with him and improve his consciousness. With their help, he can then move on to higher levels of awareness and, of course, personal improvement.

According to this theory God is in the whole reincarnation process. He works with each evolving person and with everyone together.

Henry Rucker has an entire lecture in which he explains how he evolved through a process of reincarnation. He began at first as a sunspot. Then, by becoming sand, then grass, then an animal, he finally became a man. It was a long process because he had to travel from planet to planet learning how to "be."

He learned his love feelings while he was on Venus. He learned about courage on Mars. His brains came while he was on Mercury.

In becoming a man, he first was given an "astral body," which was his emotional body. He did not yet have a physical body. All this time, he says, God was teaching him as he moved him from place to place. And, of course, Rucker admits that he is still learning about God. He feels God, because he knew him before he had a body.

Next, he got his "etheric" body, which was like a magnetic shield surrounding him. The "etheric" body is his energy body, and it came to him while he was on the moon. Finally, he came to earth for training in his physical body. According to Rucker, some of us are in training now in our physical bodies. Others are here as teachers, to help the rest of us get accustomed to our new bodies. We are always finding out what we will be eventually. God is always teaching us.

Rucker says, "We learn to feel God. We send him love by doing and being what he is." And he adds, "God has taken me over. I know he has taken me over."

He, too, emphasizes the much repeated reincarnationists' theme: "There is plenty of time to grow and get older with God. After we leave this body (by death), we will collect another body. So, don't worry, there are many reincarnations."

He explains that someday we will go to the next grade above this world and be a "man-god." We will look the same, but we will have more power. The next promotion after that is to "god-man." During both of these promotions we will be busy helping other people grow. Finally, we will come back as a god.

"God is good," says Rucker. "And we are extensions of God. He is never too busy to concern himself with us."

Rucker concludes his lecture by telling his audience that all of us are going to find God. We are like spokes and God is the hub and we are all moving toward him. We are different, but we are never right or wrong. We are all going the same way.

"I am God; so is he," says Rucker, pointing to a man in the audience. "And, together we make all of God. But we are different so that we can help each other. Our differences are meant for each other; God divides himself into us."

Although they will use some parts of the Bible, if they can fit it into what they believe, reincarnationists obviously ignore other parts: ". . . it is appointed for men to die once, and after that comes judgment" (Hebrews 9:27).

SATAN WORSHIP

The out-and-out commitment to Satan, blood pacts, calling Satan "lord and god," the belief in the teachings of *The Satanic Bible,* and the rejection of Judeo-Christian morality are some of the elements of the occult that come together in the worship and adoration of Satan.

True satanists boast that theirs is the oldest of all religions. They point to the Garden of Eden as their starting place.

Satan is the prince of demons with great power. People who worship Satan have marveled at what he has done for their lives. "I really have everything I have ever wanted, since I started serving Satan," said one satanist. He is probably right; Satan worshipers do seem to have "more" than the average person.

Jesus never denied the power of Satan; neither should the Christian. The power is there, and so is Satan's possession of the person to whom he gives his power.

Christians should know that Satanic worship is not just a religious voyeurism for those who like to see nude girls on the altar. Neither is it just a form of anti-establishment or anti-church sensationalism. Churches of Satan are forming all over the world. Within these churches are people who honor Satan as God and sincerely celebrate the power of Satan in their surrendered lives. (See Chapter 7, "The God of This World.")

SCIENCE OF MIND

"You can't equate the metaphysical, like Science of Mind, with the occult. They are different!"

That's what many people think, especially those who appreciate some of the ideas taught by the Science of Mind, or one of the other Religious Science metaphysical groups.

Metaphysics, in its formalized religious teachings, encourages man to reach out toward the unknown. It is a self-improving, self-actualizing religion that enables man to form his own beliefs about God and the Creation quite apart from any form of divine revelation. They certainly do not think that they need Jesus as the Son of God who "came to seek and to save the lost" (Luke 19:10).

Yet some think that they are Christian. One Science of Mind

church refers to itself as a school of esoteric Christianity. There people get sermons, such as "How to Develop Fourth-Dimensional Thinking," or a Mother's Day sermon on "Cosmic Motherhood—Your Laser Beam of Love," or "The Dynamic Power of Psychic Prayer," or "The Secret of the Hypnotist's Power."

These sermons teach that Jesus was a great lover of people, but then, it is added, so were Buddha, Martin Luther, and others. There is no distinction made between them. The concept of salvation is foreign to their understanding of Jesus. Excerpts from one particular Mind Science sermon reveal much about what they believe:

Man must work to get rid of his own impure ideas. He must develop a consciousness that attracts good, and eliminate the consciousness that attracts bad. Man must build up an aura, a protective power around himself. That power is the power of God that can flow through us. It comes into our "mental home," the home of the self. This auric light or positive magnetic field around ourselves keeps out the negative and doesn't let it come into our consciousness. And so we can improve ourselves. We are not sinful, nor have we any problems. We are pure conductors of the power of God, and if we offer no resistance to that power, it will constantly seek to express itself through the use of our own minds.

At a Science of Mind worship service, people are given "self-image activator" cards to use for "programming into the subconscious mind." It's a simple act. First a card is passed out to each member of the congregation and they are told to relax and read the card. The card has a spiritual message on it, a message that ends with the words "and so it is." By the time the congregation members have read through the message together, supposedly they have impressed it on their minds.

Then, each person is told to shut his eyes, imagine a black screen, and let the word "love" be written on that screen—slowly and perfectly. Then they absorb love, "and so it is."

"Are you Science of Mind?" a man asked a visitor one Sunday morning at a Science of Mind church. When the visitor said that he was not, the Science of Mind church member began to witness.

"Science of Mind helped me to overcome alcoholism," he said. "I overcame it by my mind, by becoming one with the laws of God." He explained his "theology": "I am a whole complete manifestation of the fullness of God."

He was practically paraphrasing his church's devotional

booklet *Creative Thought* which says, "I offer no resistance to the power of God which is constantly seeking to express itself through my use of mind."

Did he pray about his alcoholism? Not at all, because as Science of Mind teaches, "You must turn to the spiritual resources already within you; then the situation will clear."

Science of Mind teaches that you cannot take your problems to God. Praying is like asking God to run your errands for you. To ask God to take away your problems is a denial of your own mental thought. This is false reasoning. A person has to change his own thoughts.

Since God is the "Infinite Mind," explained the ex-alcoholic, the "Infinite Mind" only knows its own truth and cannot know evil or badness, or, in his case, alcoholism. Therefore God doesn't know we have a problem. And if God doesn't know that we have a problem, then the problem doesn't exist and we also should stop "knowing" that we have it and overcome it by the power of our minds.

"This makes sense to me," the Science of Mind ex-alcoholic said. "Alcoholics Anonymous told me about a loving God. I couldn't believe in that. It doesn't make sense that a God of love would give his Son to be nailed to some sticks."

Courses leading to a ministerial training degree in Science of Mind include such studies as "Bible Symbology," "Christ and the Mystic Marriage," and "The Trinity Inherent in Causation." These courses offer keys to unlock the "Code of the Bible," keys that are needed if one is going to understand the symbology, astrology, and numerology hidden in the Bible. The esoteric Bible mysteries that lead to self-fulfillment must be tapped. The courses offered in Science of Mind and Mental Cybernetics teach a person how to do it.

People who want to be Science of Mind ministers do not have to go to college or seminary. If they take the required number of courses in the School of Esoteric Christianity including: "Exploring the God Idea," "The Magic of Believing," "The Wisdom of Your Subconscious Mind," "The Art of Dream Interpretation," and "The Wisdom and Teaching Beyond Yoga," they will be graduated as "full ministers of the Gospel."

Science of Mind churches seem to draw the lonely and the confused. Those attracted are struggling to improve themselves by their own abilities and strength, yet are always lacking because they are part of their own problem. Weakness can't produce strength no matter how hard one struggles to convince himself that he is not really weak. So Science of Mind people keep trying and keep hearing encouraging words that they can do it by themselves, when, deep down inside, they know that if they could do it by themselves, they would have already done it.

Where does it all end? Do they ever know the embracing love of God that can lift them up and put them on their feet so that they can "run and not be weary . . . walk and not faint"? They are never introduced to God. Even at death, there is no God waiting. When a man dies, Science of Mind teaches that he has simply "elected the wider view of immortality." Always he is on his own. Nowhere, not even in death, does this metaphysical religion offer any hope in God.

SPIRITUALISM

Spiritualism or spiritism is a belief in spirits that can communicate to us from the spirit world. The seances of mediums are built upon the belief in living spirits who can communicate from "the other side."

There are now some 150,000 members of spiritualist churches across the United States and they continue to increase as more and more people study their relationship to the spirit world. Spiritualists are very religious and much of what they are taught is couched in Christian terminology. But they are not Christian. Officially, the National Spiritualist Association of Churches in the U.S.A. denies that there can be any Christian spiritualists. Some spiritualist groups that have branched off disagree, but they show no evidence of a biblical understanding or presentation of Jesus.

Spiritualists will not commit themselves to Jesus as the Way, the Truth, and the Life. To them, he is "a way," or "a spirit," but he is only one of many ways to come to God.

"Jesus is a brother spirit, even a greater spirit," explained a man who was once involved in the spiritualist movement. He said spiritualists believe that Jesus teaches us just as do many other spirits who have gone on teach us. He is no different from anyone else, except that those who respect him will say that he has progressed farther than most of us.

But spiritualists who are interested in developing to higher and higher planes in the spirit world will deny that Jesus has any ability to bring us into a relationship with God. Most of them cannot conceive of anyone meeting God because God, too, is evolving to greater planes. The best we can ever do is to reach a plane where God once was.

Spiritualism, as we know it today, began in the eighteenth century. Anton Mesmer may have been the first to hold a modern seance. As the people held hands in his seances, they were "magnetized" or "hypnotized" and cured of their illnesses.

Andrew Jackson Davis is reported to have been the first American spiritualist. He was born in 1826 in Blooming Grove, New York. He was a poor student, even failing as an apprentice in the shoemaker trade. Attending lectures on mesmerism, he allowed himself to be hypnotized. While he was in these hypnotic states, he demonstrated unusual clairvoyant powers. He could read a newspaper while blindfolded, or he could see into other rooms and even other houses where he had never visited.

He began to get involved in various forms of healing, using his own remedies that came to him while he was in a hypnotic trance. From that, he moved into a dimension where he claimed to be able to visit the spirit realms. He also began to teach his beliefs about God and the spirits.

Davis was opposed to the Christian faith. He did not believe in heaven or hell, but he did believe in spiritual spheres where spirits move after death. He taught that as man is in harmony with the laws of God, he naturally gravitates toward God, always moving to higher spheres but never reaching an end, or an arrival in the presence of God.

Spiritualism spread fairly rapidly in America. Even though the Fox sisters admitted their "tappings" were a fraud, many who followed them claimed to have experienced contact with the spirit world. After 1850 there were many mediums in the United States and abroad who claimed that they could communicate with the spirit world by tapping, automatic writing, or directly through speech.

Some people make a distinction between spiritualism and spiritism and are distressed when the two are referred to together. Spiritists make contact with the spirit world, without making the practice a part of religious belief. Spiritualists, on the other hand, have a religious framework for their belief in spirits and the contacting of spirits. The practices of both, however, are basically the same.

There are several branches of spiritualists. Like Protestant denominations, they differ over some aspects of their religious beliefs.

The spiritualists first began to associate together in the National Spiritualist Association of Churches in the United States of America in 1893. This "mainline" group of spiritualists has tried to bring some order out of a widely divergent group of spiritualist churches that sprang up somewhat independently of each other.

They now have a type of seminary, the Morris-Pratt Institute, in Milwaukee, Wisconsin. A person must have been active in a spiritualist church and proven himself before he is allowed to study there and improve his powers as a medium. He is not ordained until he is examined by the National Board. Some in the Association disagree with the idea of a seminary, feeling that the information comes from God and does not require an education or special spiritualistic instruction.

A few spiritualist churches in the Association have tried to have Sunday school for children, but most children are not interested in the spirit world or communication with people who have died.

The Spiritualist Science Church, which was founded in 1923, stresses healing. Disagreeing with the National Spiritualist Association of Churches in the U.S.A., they believe that spiritualism and Christianity do go together and emphasize the work of Jesus in their ministry of healing. However, they do not go far enough with Jesus to trust in him as Savior. For them, salvation comes through the process of being cleansed through prayer.

The Independent Spiritualist Association, founded in 1924, is basically in accord with the larger NSA, but allows its followers to believe in reincarnation, a position not held by all in the NSA.

The Aquarian Brotherhood of Christ, founded in 1925, puts stress on man's relationship to God and his right to call on Christ. One leader said that making the sign of the cross will bring advanced spirits. But she wasn't really trusting Jesus; she was calling on him to give her the additional help she needed to contact the spirit world. She wasn't interested in biblical revelation either. She said God sent his messages to her directly.

The Universal Spiritualist Association, founded in 1956, denies Christian teachings such as the sin of man and his need for cleansing through Jesus Christ. Members of this group teach that man was conceived immaculate, just like Jesus. Interpreting the Bible their own way, they also teach that man is immortal as proven by the resurrection of Jesus.

Spiritualists believe that there are spirits all around. They are on the earth plane and they are in the spirit world. They are everywhere. All men have spirits. These spirits are ongoing; they never end. It is logical, to the spiritualists, that spirits can be contacted on the "other side." It is no different than communicating with men here. For them, the natural world and the spirit world are much alike. Sometimes a spirit is on earth in a man and we talk to him; other times he is on "the other side," so we talk to him there. The spirit can communicate no matter which world he is in.

Christians often get very frustrated talking to spiritualists. They use the same words, but mean two different things. It is hard to talk about the soul or spirit that God breathed into man as always existing, and not sound like a spiritualist. Christians and spiritualists part company on the issues of salvation through Jesus Christ and on the definitions of heaven and hell. At that point the Christian is seen as "too narrow." The spiritualist sees orthodox Christianity as somehow limiting God. He does not understand that the Christian is not putting restrictions on God by saying what God will and will not do, but he is simply accepting the explanation that God gives in Scripture about the ways that He will act.

Spiritualists want a "God force," one who holds the planets together in their orbits and makes them move in conjunction. They speak of God as the One who holds people together and makes them move in order, too. They see man as a part of the whole nature of things. They explain God as "Infinite Intelligence." So, man must live in harmony with this Infinite Intelligence if he is going to be balanced physically, mentally and spiritually.

"But that's what we believe, too," says the Christian, trying to discover some common frame of reference with the spiritualist.

He soon finds out, however, that what the spiritualist is saying is not what Christians believe. The spiritualist works at this harmony with the Infinite Intelligence by his own power, guided and directed from the spirit world. His coming into harmony with the Infinite Intelligence has been an ongoing process for a long time. He has never had a beginning; he has always been in the process; and he will never have an ending either.

To the spiritualist, life is made up of vibrations. The spiritual matter and the physical matter are simply different forms of vibration, one higher than the other. Vibrations never end; so spiritualists can learn a great deal about people from their vibrations. Through "psychometry" a medium can touch an object and tell something about the owner of that object. Since everyone supposedly has vibrations, they leave their vibrations, like fingerprints, on everything that they touch. These vibrations can reveal illness, life, death, or the whereabouts of someone.

Even a photograph of a person has an aura or vibration to it. The spirit of that person is vibrating, because whether he is on this earth or on "the other side," his spirit exists. When a medium touches an object left behind by someone who has disappeared, he can tell immediately whether that person is alive or dead. The vibrations are different, depending on whether the spirit is here or on "the other side" in the spirit world. This aura, or vibration, is real enough to cause Russian scientists to label the sensing of it "skin vision."

Those who prophesy, like Jeane Dixon, claim to be sensitive to vibrations in other existences so that they can sense things in other dimensions that have not yet entered or materialized into our dimension. They interpret the aura or the vibrations around someone and know in advance what is going to happen. Jeane Dixon claims to have known in advance the place in the hotel kitchen where Robert Kennedy was shot. The vibrations were very strong to her, but she could not convince the Kennedy family. Successes like hers convince many people to seek out psychics and spiritualists for advice.

Spiritualist ministers not only attempt to guide a person by the information that they receive from the spirits, but they also offer healing. This healing power is defined as a force that comes out of them. The healing dimension of spiritualism is gaining a lot of interest in other occult groups.

Contact with spirits, the ability to give instructions from the spirit world, and the power to heal bring a lot of respect to the professional spiritualist. He will rarely share his spiritual insights publicly. Guidance is usually given in private, which means no one really knows if he is receiving personal spirit guidance or the same message that was given to the person who left the church just ahead of him. Not only do the guiding ministers in spiritualism tend to keep their followers from hearing the guidance given to another, but they keep their followers away from other spiritualist clergy as well. Referrals are unheard of. Telephone a spiritualist minister and somewhere in the conversation (while he is trying to encourage you to come in for a "reading") he will let you know that he is "better" or has "been at it longer" than the other spiritualist ministers in the same city.

"They are jealous of one another," said a man who left the movement. He feels that they are not really interested in guiding or helping people; they are only interested in building a large personal following. He also commented that the "beliefs" expressed to people by the departed spirits are always the same as the beliefs held by the spiritualist minister.

There are even ministers of Christian congregations who are involved in spiritualism. Victor H. Ernest, author of *I Talked with Spirits*, refers to ministers who use the "spirit messages" that they have received for their Sunday sermons. These messages are always based on the moral or ethical teachings of Jesus, never on his being the Christ, the Son of the living God.[5]

Before he died, Arthur Ford, who began his career as a minister in Kentucky, taught the benefits of spiritualism to Christian ministers and laymen. He put great emphasis on the spirit power that is available to churches.

Because many who rely on the spirits assume that they are working in conjunction with the spirit of man and the nature of God, they will sometimes use the term "Christian spiritualism" to describe their religious practice. But this term is deceptive. "Christ" to them is the "Christ Spirit" who is within everyone. By following the Christ Spirit, a person can improve himself. The Christ Spirit is a teaching spirit, not Jesus Christ the Savior.

Spiritualism deepens the prayer life of a Christian, according to spiritualist believers. Therefore people ought to get into spiritualism and receive from the spirits the depth that they need in their praying. Since this praying opens doors to such additional spiritual gifts as wisdom and healing, contact with the spirits is obviously Christian, the spiritualist argument continues.

There are poorly taught Christian people who get caught by this line of reasoning. They also tend to accept the spiritualist

[5] Victor H. Ernest, *I Talked with Spirits* (Wheaton. Ill.: Tyndale House Publishers, 1971), p. 38.

reasoning that since we have been created by God and have eternal life, and God is alive and we pray to God, then it makes sense that we can also talk to the people who have eternal life on "the other side."

Spiritualism is an attempt to "prove" life after death, but it ignores the biblical teaching about life after death. It substitutes a survival of the soul theory for eternal life.

When those critical of spiritualism say that you can't call people back from the dead—if they are dead, you cannot talk to them— the spiritualist replies: "Is he really dead? He only appears to be dead, but there is a spirit of immortality in him. He is really alive. So, it isn't difficult or strange to talk to someone who is alive."

To deny the influence of spiritism and spiritualism on people, even within the Christian church, is to be blind. Victor Ernest, in the Preface of his book *I Talked with Spirits*, quotes from Thomson J. Hudson who wrote in the *Law of Psychic Phenomena*: "A man who denies the phenomena of spiritism today is not entitled to be called a skeptic, he is simply ignorant."

People who have had experiences with spiritualism, and then come out of it to Jesus Christ, do not deny the power of spiritualism. Their personal involvement has proven to them that it is possible to communicate with spirits. But they also know the Satanic control and manipulation in spiritualism and they speak with great fear and concern for those who are still in it.

TAROT CARDS

Tarot cards, like astrology, are used by a person to find guidance for his life. By the cards he makes decisions that he expects will help him to move in harmony with the universal order. This approach is based on the assumption that everything that exists has an astrological correspondence and a tarot card association. To understand the tarot, a person must understand astrology. The tarot is called a silver key to unlock secrets. In order to manipulate the tarot, a person also needs the golden key of astrology.

Together, astrology and the tarot are used to explain symbolically the secrets of man. Tarot believers say that the subconscious mind knows a lot more about the symbolic nature of man than most people realize. They use the tarot cards to explain the universal language that reveals the secrets of their lives and the world around them. Hence, a person casts the cards to know what decisions to make. He uses the tarot cards to find out how his life should be lived.

People are desperate for order and direction in their lives, particularly many young people. One young man said, "I wouldn't go anywhere without my tarot cards. I wouldn't want to make an important decision without them." The cards govern the tarot believer's thinking, and they work the following way:

The seventy-eight illustrated cards are divided into the Major and Minor Arcana. The fifty-six Minor Arcana cards have four suits: cups, swords, pentacles, and wands. The twenty-two Major Arcana cards are symbolic.

After the cards are shuffled, with some cards pulled out or allowed to fall out, the top fifteen cards are ready to be read. To insure a good reading, the reader blows on the cards, repeats over them the name of the person for whom they are being read, and, if possible, has the inquirer touch the cards.

The reader then chooses a card layout. There are many layouts for different situations. As the cards are shuffled, cut, and spread, everyone concentrates on the question being asked. This concentration of energy on the cards causes the cards to fall correctly. By concentrating, the power generated also helps the subconscious understand the meaning of the cards.

The meaning of the cards is derived not so much from their face value as from their position in relationship to each other. The cards "tell" the inquirer what he needs to know so that he can act accordingly, knowing that he has been given direction that will keep him in harmony with the whole universal order. In other words, he acts with the confidence that he is in the "will" of the cosmic whole.

Much of what the cards tell is discovered through feeling. They seem to give off "cool" or "hot" or "prickly" feelings. These feelings are attributed to the vibrations in the cards which come from the person concentrating on them. The assumption that everyone radiates, or gives off vibrations, is based on the motion or continuous energy theory that is a part of so much of occult thinking. These radiations or emanations are believed to put vibrations or power within the cards. The person's vibration or magnetism is then felt by the reader as he touches and studies the cards.

Tarot believers teach that the mind must be disciplined to obey the directions that are given by the tarot. The mind must not argue or question the reading, but be ready to follow the orders given by the cards. "Truth" will come from the cards; the recipient must be prepared to follow that "truth" if it is going to do him any good.

The tarot is old. Some historians place its beginnings in the fourteenth century. However, books on the tarot written by believers claim that there is an older form of the cards that dates back 35,000 years.

Believers in the tarot see the cards as very important for the proper development of modern man. They lament the "spiritual decay" brought on by man's study of the physical sciences. This empirical study has cut out some of the ancient spiritual answers about life that man hungers for. Modern man's soul is left with a need. Users of the tarot cards explain that this "soul need" can be met by investigation of the spiritual dimensions of life through the cards.

TELEPATHY

Telepathy is the ability to hear the thinking of another person or the ability to discern and communicate messages over great distances. As in other types of ESP, telepathy has been tested and proven. Some people have a definite telepathic ability to hear messages sent by others.

Frederic W. H. Meyers first coined the word "telepathy" before the turn of the century. Telepathy, unlike clairvoyance, requires a sender. The thought in one person's mind can be projected to another person's mind. Some people link telepathy to a form of precognition. However, precognition seems to be a "knowing" of the sender's thoughts even before he thinks them.

The existence, as such, of telepathy should not bother Christians. They know that there are many dimensions and abilities in man. What does bother Christians is, "Who owns the mind that sends or receives the messages?" Christians have already decided to "take every thought captive to obey Christ" (2 Corinthians 10:5) and take seriously the scriptural teaching "Be transformed by the renewal of your mind, that you may prove what is the will of God, what is good and acceptable and perfect" (Romans 12:2).

WITCHCRAFT

There are two forms of witchcraft—black and white. White

witchcraft supposedly brings good to people. It is meant to be healing and helpful. But one white witch may have spoken for others, too, when she said, "I'm not above using a little black magic if it will keep my enemies off my back."

For black witches, anything that is normally considered good is bad, anything considered bad is good. They openly attribute their powers to Satan, but they do not think of him as the Devil. To them he is a benevolent power who will give them the abilities and powers that they need so long as they acknowledge him as the giver of these "good gifts."

The word "witch" comes from the word "wit," which means to know. "Wiccas" is an Old English word for wise ones. They practice their cult as a religion that is built around the attempt to harness or use the powers in the world. Witches cast spells, make magic potions, and channel the energy in vibrations. The *Book of Shadows* is known as the witches' bible. The *Gospel of the Witches* contains prayers, incantations, and hymns.

The ritual of a witches' sabbat is both the worship of nature and the enjoyment of a person's own sensual feelings. Witches worship the earth goddess and the vibrations that come from each other. Dancing around an altar, often outdoors, sometimes naked, begins with a follow-the-leader-type dance that moves into a slow-moving, side-stepping circling with hands joined. The dance gives an exciting feeling of being close to nature and to each other. At the May Eve celebration, nude dancing has traditionally been practiced. But since it is not required at any other celebration, even this tradition is being dropped as witchcraft increases in popularity.

The Grand Master of a "coven," or group of witches, is always a man, sometimes still called "Devil." Although many covens are ruled by the priestess, the male witch is still "lord." Only non-witches call male witches "warlocks." Witches never use that term. The coven consists of thirteen people who make up the "Boucca's Dozen" or "Devil's Dozen." "Boucca" is an old Celtic word for god or spirit. The familiar term "baker's dozen" may well have come from this old witches' term.

Witches, both black and white, are said to have a high susceptibility to mental depression. Dabbling in magic, dealing with spells, and even their dependency on "forces" seem to overwhelm many of them with a lack of peace. In their efforts to help others, even "good" witches lose their own calm and stability. Few, however, would admit to the possibility of demon possession.

People who have been trained in witchcraft, particularly the black arts, have saturated their lives with evil and hate. This hatred soon becomes an illness that gets into every part of them. One old witch said of herself, "I have never been able to love. I can't love."

From this survey of various forms of the occult, the reader will have noted certain basic beliefs. Different approaches are taken, different emphases are put upon these beliefs in different occult practices; but always there are the common, familiar threads running through—the ability of the spirit to transcend space and time, the ability to communicate with spirits and/or supernatural powers, and the existence of a pattern of harmonious vibrations in the universe, and the need for man to live in harmony with these patterns.

Unlike the major religions, the occult is not systematized. Anyone can be part of it. He can call himself by many names and fit somewhere into the occult. What does seem to be consistent, however, is the religious appeal of the occult and its use of "almost Christian" terminology. Whereas a Christian would never give up his faith in Christ, join another major religion, and continue to refer to himself as a Christian, many do continue to think of themselves as Christian as they drift into the occult. By adjusting their convictions a little bit here, or "adding" a little there to the meaning of their faith, they are soon practicing occult religious beliefs while convinced that they are "improved Christians." The drift into the occult is always called a "liberating" or "deepening" or "enlarging" experience. This characteristic is Satan's way. He has never yet told the truth. As an "angel of light" he has a lot to give, but then he has a lot to gain by giving.

There are many "good" people in the occult who are personally very religious. Although some occult people gravitate to the extreme of satanism, most want to "serve God." For them, Satan offers his slightly adjusted "Christianity." For the people who have drifted or are drifting into the occult, there have been provided well-qualified teachers as guides. Most of these teachers are not even aware of the responsible positions they hold as rulers of the shadows.

Rulers of the Shadows

"I've been a witch since I was twelve," said Jeffrey Cather of Toledo, in a *Toledo Blade* interview, April 2, 1972. "I am a traditional witch, my great-grandmother was a witch and so were several ancestors."

Not to be outdone by anybody, Sybil Leek claims that her family's involvement in the craft can be traced farther back than anybody else's.

Whether they have sought after occult leadership, or simply accepted the mantle that has fallen upon them, most teachers and leaders of the occult can trace a family heritage in the esoteric beliefs. They may differ in attitude, conviction, method, and life-style, but most of the people who today are in popular demand as occult leaders were in the crafts before the current revival. And their claim to have a direct relationship with earlier generations is a little frightening.

"Yes," said a West Coast woman, "both my mother and grandmother had psychic powers."

"What about your great-grandmother?" asked a concerned Christian, thinking of God's injunction and the accompanying threat:

> You shall have no other gods before me. You shall not make for yourself a graven image, or any likeness of anything that is in heaven above, or that is in the earth beneath, or that is in the water under the earth; you shall not bow down to them or serve them; for I the Lord your God am a jealous God, visiting the iniquity of the fathers upon the children to the third and the fourth generation of those who hate me (Exodus 20:3-5).

"I don't think so," she replied. "But my daughter is definitely psychic."

A brief examination of the lives and mission of a few occult leaders reveals both the person and something of the scope of the occult movement.

Using his powers of clairvoyance and healing, and with his special training in the arts of witchcraft, England's *Alex Sanders* claims to be the most powerful witch in Europe. In 1965, 1,623 witches crowned him "King of the Witches," a title last held by Owain Glyndwr in the fifteenth century. As the leader of 107 covens, he would seem to be an appropriate holder of the title.

Sanders' grandmother marked him as a witch when he was still a little boy. She declared that she would kill him if he ever gave away her secrets. From that time on, Sanders knew the forces of witchcraft. As a young man, he demanded that his demons bring him power, wealth, and pleasure, and he did receive them.

His developing years saw him moving back and forth between the excitement of being able to work magic power for himself, and the loneliness of not being able to find other witches. Finally, giving up his wealth, he dedicated himself to a serious study of the witch's arts. Like a missionary in training, he studied and practiced his craft, preparing for the time when there would be others in his coven. When the day came when witchcraft was no longer ridiculed but became a respectable and sought after occult belief, he was ready.

His work began in earnest after a nine-day fast and a three-day purification rite. He described the climax of that rite as a giddy feeling accompanied by a sound of rushing air. Letters appeared in the sand in front of him listing the names of special spirits. When he called upon the spirits, a voice responded telling him that he would share witchcraft with the world. This experience was his commissioning, and he began to look for others to teach.

The first persons to become his pupils were a devout "Christian" couple whom Sanders describes as the "revivalist" type. They were already interested in talking with angels; so they were open to his teachings about witchcraft. They thought witchcraft would help them to improve their communication with the angels. With this beginning, the group expanded as Sanders brought an increasing number of initiates into the craft.

Sanders' life is a study in commitment. He believes that even his marriage to Maxine, a seventeen-year-old witch, was revealed to him first through his crystal ball and then through his "familiar" who searched out the future for him. No one could criticize Sanders for consciously trying to deceive others. His whole life gives witness to the reality of his belief in witchcraft and its power in the life of a dedicated person.

To Sanders, witchcraft is compatible with any other religion. His initiates have never been brought into witchcraft casually. He believes that witchcraft is a religion of requirements. He has even held back from teaching witchcraft to people whom he did not consider to be ready. When his people gather in a coven, they are committed to what they are doing. Their religion is not a game and their devil (a type of "assistant angel") is alive.

There have been several other notable witches in Britain. Before Alex Sanders, *Gerald Gardner* was the best-known English witch. He is considered by men like Sanders to have been a "novice"-type witch. That is, he was properly initiated into the first grade of witchcraft but didn't bother going through to the third grade. He just went ahead and recruited other followers, a practice which disturbed the careful Sanders.

Gardner bypassed many of the hereditary witches' rituals and devised some of his own. He took credit for organizing the witches' "Cone of Power" that some believe to have stopped Hitler from crossing the English Channel. Before he died, Gardner established a Witchcraft Museum on the Isle of Man.

Aleister Crowley was born in 1875. This English witch thought of himself as the reincarnation of a French Roman Catholic priest/ witch / spiritualist / magician who died the year Crowley was born.

Crowley used witchcraft to gain personal power and to satisfy his own lusts, and soon he was calling himself the most wicked man in the world. Writers describe his mother's conviction that she had given birth to the Great Beast (666) of Revelation. He used heroin, called himself a messiah, and used the rituals of witchcraft to suit himself. Still, before he died in 1947, he had developed a fairly sizable following.

One of the best-known witches is *Sybil Leek,* who was born in England but teaches and writes in the United States. As a "full-time" witch, she has popularized witchcraft for the masses. She writes books on spells, magic potions, and other do-it-in-the-privacy-of-your-own-home types of witches' magic that supposedly will help even the beginner have a good time with witchcraft.

It all seems to be fun for Sybil Leek. She doesn't communicate the strong religious feelings about witchcraft that are so much a part of the teachings of witches like Alex Sanders. For her, witchcraft is almost a game, to be enjoyed by everybody. She doesn't emphasize the source of witch power or the serious personal commitment that First-, Second-, and Third-Degree witches acknowledge. She claims that large numbers speak or write to her weekly about their interest in witchcraft. She enjoys telling them about the great "adventure" of witchcraft. She doesn't tell them about the demonic world and gets very angry at evangelical Christians who write letters to her telling her that she is leading people into the grip of Satan.

Louise Huebner is known as the honorary witch of Los Angeles, a title conferred upon her by Ernest E. Debs, Chairman of the Board of County Supervisors. She received the title one night at a Folklore Festival in the Hollywood Bowl. She was asked to cast "the world's largest spell." So she did, casting a spell to increase sexual vitality in the county.

Mrs. Huebner, who lives with her husband and three children, calls herself a "good witch." She does radio shows and speaks to college and university audiences on astrology, numerology, witchcraft, and telepathy. She vies with Sybil Leek for the honor of being the greatest witch. Both have a mass appeal through their teaching, writing, and activities as witches.

The Reverend *Arthur Ford* was one of America's most famous psychic mediums. People like Sir Arthur Conan Doyle and Bishop James A. Pike called upon him to contact the spirit world. Pike felt that Ford enabled him to contact his son Jim who had committed suicide. Through the work of Ford as a medium, Pike became a firm believer in life "on the other side."

In February, 1928, in his home in New York, Ford announced that he had broken the famous Houdini code. Houdini had arranged this code for communication from the spirit world. The code was to be a test of a medium's ability and a test whether or not spirits could communicate after a person had died. At first, Ford was praised as a great medium for having broken the code. Then there began to come charges that he had, in fact, been given the code by Houdini's family. These charges and his denials went on for ten years. He was temporarily suspended from the United Spiritualists' League, but it didn't matter. By then, the publicity had brought him enough notoriety to launch him as a popular medium.

Ford taught the immortality of the soul but really meant a type of recycling of souls. He believed that souls go into the spirit world when they "die" and then return when babies are "born." Some stay on "the other side" longer than others, depending on what interesting work they are doing in the spirit world or how much they just enjoy the freedom of their astral existence.

According to Ford, a proper understanding of psychic phenomena would help to clear out mental hospitals. He felt that many people are controlled by obsessions that are related to psychic experiences, but labeled as mental illness. Some contemporary scientists in the United States and Russia, who in no way pretend to be mediums like Ford, are having some of the same thoughts as Ford about the causes of mental illness.

Ford was one of the leaders in the early days of the Spiritual Frontiers Fellowship. His interest, like that of SFF today, was in promoting an awareness of psychic consciousness in churches. What he was promoting, however, was not Christianity but spiritualism. Ford was a particularly able spokesman for SFF since he, like other leaders in SFF, was an ordained clergyman. His Christian (Disciples) background gave him the theological language he needed to talk about spirit existence to church people.

Ford was quite successful with some ministers. Apparently spiritualism, reincarnation, and astral existence have a certain appeal to the clergyman who has always had a little trouble believing in heaven and hell. The self-improvement motif that is part of the attraction of reincarnation seems to appeal to many people who are cultural Christians.

On California Street in San Francisco there stands a three-storied house painted entirely black. The windows on the lower floors are all shuttered. A high steel fence backed by wooden slats blocks the view of the curious. A black Toronado is parked in front, bearing California license plates with the letters VAMPYR. It is the home of *Anton Szandor LaVey*, the "Black Pope." He lives there with his wife and two daughters and also conducts Satanic worship there for the church members who pay the required entrance fee.

Visitors are not allowed. Some national magazine writers have been received into his home, but others, especially those doing religious or sociological research, are not.

"He doesn't like all of that publicity," commented one frustrated visitor. But his actions seem to belie any shyness. He has invited the press to weddings and to the "baptism" of his own daughter, and he seems to enjoy the national coverage that is given to his naked "altars" that titillate the public. He seems to like the pictures taken of himself also.

"He doesn't want to be exposed," said another who was barred from joining the Church of Satan. But there isn't anything to expose about LaVey's beliefs; he is openly a worshiper of Satan. What might be exposed are some of his shock-value trappings, like the stuffed rat that leers at visitors or the bookcase that swings open to reveal a sinister-looking inner sanctum. Even this kind of circus stuff gets old if seen too often.

LaVey began his career in a circus. He quit high school in his junior year to join the Clyde Beatty Circus, first as a cage boy and then as an assistant trainer of the cats. He moved up to calliope player and then quit the circus to join a carnival. While he worked at the carnival, he began to observe the inconsistency in people. He claims that he watched men lusting after the burlesque girls on Saturday night and sitting with their families in evangelistic tent meetings on Sunday. He began to think about the need for honest worship, where the flesh is openly exalted and people seek their pleasure openly, instead of doing it secretly while maintaining the trappings of Christian devotion.

When he married, he became a police photographer. As he took pictures of dead bodies, knifed and shot, and saw some of the wretched things that people did to others, he "knew" that there couldn't be a God. He was becoming more certain that life was raw and people were base and that honesty meant admitting the reality of evil, not "sanctimoniously" calling on God.

He quit his job, went back to playing the organ, this time in nightclubs, and formed a magic group. By now he was completing his satanist education. He had learned that the world was Darwinian in that there was a dog-eat-dog struggle with everyone taking and clawing. He had found no evidence of a loving God involved in people's lives.

His magic group was the forerunner of his Church of Satan. He was learning that there were results from Satan worship that he couldn't lightly dismiss as coincidence. The group quickly outgrew their first interest in mocking and ridiculing the Christian church. In Satan worship they were discovering a lot more than they had anticipated. LaVey and his group began to believe that their worship of Satan was giving them what they wanted and that their lives were demonstrating a force that assured them that Satan was helping them.

On May Eve, or Walpurgisnacht, 1966, when he was thiry-six years old, LaVey shaved his head, put on a clerical collar, and dedicated his Church of Satan. His announced purpose was to combine outrage and respectability. He wanted like-minded people to meet together to call up the Satanic powers that he knew from experience were available. And he wanted a church of pleasure where human indulgence would be part of the ritual. To him, people should go to church to find pleasure instead of (as he saw it) leaving the dry worship of an austere church to go out and find pleasure elsewhere.

Many agree with LaVey. Since 1966, Churches of Satan have sprung up all over the United States. The San Francisco church alone claims 10,000 members, but others in Kentucky, Michigan, Ohio, and New York are growing rapidly.

When people answer newspaper ads for an *Edgar Cayce* Study Group forming in their area, they are invited to discussion meetings that stress dreams and reincarnation as part of coming into a whole life pattern of doing good.

The late Edgar Cayce, referred to by many as a devout Christian (he was a Sunday school teacher and is said to have read his Bible through every year), was the founder of these study groups that are spreading everywhere. He was known as "the sleeping prophet," because while in a trance he gave directions to thousands of people. He listed over 2,000 instances of diagnosing illnesses and prescribing medication successfully. He was so popular that the Association of Research and Enlightenment in Virginia Beach carries on his programs today.

Although *Time* magazine, March 21, 1969, called *Carroll Righter* "the best-known and most successful of U.S. astrologers," and titled him "dean of America's public astrologers," he does not compare in overall popularity with prophetess Jeane Dixon. Righter publishes his astrological information in 306 newspapers reaching 30 million American homes. And, *Time* reports, he is making very good money at it.

But *Jeane Dixon,* even without the showmanship of astrologer Maurice Woodruff who airs his predictions over British syndicated television, has developed a following that listens to her with near reverence. Jeane Dixon declares that her gift of prophecy comes from God. But she stresses astrology, visions, and vibrations more than the revelation that God has already given in Scripture. Those who write about her do not question her ethics, morals, or honesty. She is a genuine and sincere person. And with great sincerity she claims the same revelation of God through her gifts today that the prophets claimed long ago. As Isaiah, Ezekiel, and Daniel had their message for their day, she has her message for today; then and now, she says, the source is God.

She bases her convictions about her prophetic gifts on the teaching of Scripture. In Numbers 12:6 God said he would make himself known to a prophet in visions and dreams. He spoke in that way to Daniel (7:1) and to Hosea (12:10) and told Amos that "Surely the Lord God does nothing, without revealing his secret to his servants the prophets" (3:7). In 2 Kings 22:14-15 Hilkiah the priest received the Word of God from Huldah the prophetess. Mrs. Dixon uses these passages to explain her own prophetic gifts but does not use Scripture to point people to God.

Recognizing that a prophet must be a servant of God, Mrs. Dixon claims two important biblical passages for her life and prophecy. In her book *My Life and Prophecies,* as told to Rene Noorbergen,[1] she refers to Deuteronomy 13:1-4 and 1 John 4:2:

"If a prophet arises among you, or a dreamer of dreams, and gives you a sign or a wonder, and the sign or wonder which he tells you comes to pass, and if he says, 'Let us go after other gods,' which you have not known, and 'let us serve them,' you shall not listen to the words of that prophet or to that dreamer of dreams; for the Lord your God is testing you, to know whether you love the Lord your God with all your heart and with all your soul. You shall walk after the Lord your God and fear him, and keep his commandments and obey his voice, and you shall serve him and cleave to him."

By this you know the Spirit of God: every spirit which confesses that Jesus Christ has come in the flesh is of God.

[1] Jeane Dixon, *My Life and Prophecies,* edited by Rene Noorbergen (New York: William Morrow & Co., 1969), pp. 15-16.

Concerned Christians, conscious of her impact on people, keep asking themselves, "If she believes that people should serve God and believes that Jesus Christ has come in the flesh, why doesn't she urge people to commit themselves to God and why doesn't she also proclaim the death, resurrection, and redeeming ministry of Jesus?"

But she skirts all but the ethical teachings of the Bible, preferring to emphasize her own prophecy and a form of universalism that is somehow, someday going to draw all men to God. She skips over the "narrow way" that Jesus taught, preferring the broad way that Jeane Dixon teaches, while all the time calling her way the teaching of Jesus. In so doing she has become very popular and has won many friends.

One day in 1967 at the Belgian Embassy in Washington, D.C., a white dove flew in the window during a ceremony honoring one of Mrs. Dixon's friends. As she held the white dove in her hand, she had a vision of a "Blazing Cross of Christ" coming into the Eastern sky. This cross, she was told, would appear in the year 1999. She took it as God's statement to her that everyone in the world would someday be his disciple. Hindu, Jew, and Buddhist would all be his. This prospect is probably upsetting to the Hindus, Jews, and Buddhists, who do not want to be disciples of Jesus, but it does please the many semi-Christian people who like the idea that someday all faiths will be united in what Mrs. Dixon calls "the brotherhood of Christ."

There was also another side to this prediction. She spoke of a time of judgment for all humanity and added her feeling that destruction was coming. She described the rise of a great war lord who will masquerade as a peacemaker. She saw a great war coming between the East and West, fought east of the Jordan River. All of these events, she predicted, will occur between 1999 and the 2030's. They will be preceded by great earthquakes and tidal waves, caused by a comet striking the earth in the 1980's.

Many biblically oriented Christians who also look for the glorious return of Jesus agree that an attractive anti-Christ, earthquakes, and wars will all be part of the great end time. Many expect these events to occur soon and have no trouble accepting Mrs. Dixon's prophecies. Much of what she says is in line with traditional Christian thought.

When Mrs. Dixon speaks of Satan's attempt to seduce the world by encouraging men to follow human knowledge alone, many Christians agree. She explains that the forerunner of the anti-Christ will prepare the world for Satan. Many Christians agree. She states that this prophetic forerunner was born on February 5, 1962, in the Middle East. He will lead the world away from Jesus Christ. He will appear to be very Christlike himself; yet he will deceive the world in the name and power of Satan. Quoting 1 John 2:22, she calls the anti-Christ a liar. Most Christians have no argument with that either. She tells of unusual miracles and signs in the last days that will lead men astray. Again, many Christians agree. She urges people to prepare themselves for some great spiritual battles that are coming. Once again, Christians agree with her.

The events explained by Mrs. Dixon's prophecies are not so troubling to Christians. Most agree that what she says is consistent with their interpretation of prophecy. What does trouble these Christians is that she summarizes her prophecies with the prediction that all men will stand before God as disciples. She gets close to Christian teaching and then veers to one side, refusing to call men and women to Christ. Instead, she gives a false hope of security about man's final stand before God, ignoring the biblical teaching that emphasizes that when persons stand before God, he will be either Redeemer or Judge. Her universalism negates the terrible price of Calvary. If Jeane Dixon is correct now, then God was wrong at the crucifixion two thousand years ago. If God intended to wink at the sin that put Jesus on the cross, why the cross? Although most universalists will teach the cross, saying that Jesus died for the world therefore the world is saved, Mrs. Dixon doesn't even go that far. Her Christology seems to go only as far as Jesus coming in the flesh.

Christians examining the words of Jeane Dixon must ponder whether she has a gift of prophecy from God or Satan. She believes that Jesus has come in the flesh, so does Satan. She believes that he is coming again. Certainly Satan believes that, too, thus the spiritual warfare that is coming. Satan, knowing the facts of God's plan far better than men, can and will twist the meaning of God's revelation. He is and always has been a deceiver. The way that Mrs. Dixon parallels Scripture, and yet refuses to emphasize the redemptive message of Scripture, frightens the Christians who read their Bibles and captivates those who don't.

Many people are offended at any questioning of Mrs. Dixon's standing with God. She claims to be totally opposed to Satan and claims allegiance to God. She also prays regularly at her church. Thus, many believe that she is a committed Christian; yet she doesn't say that she is committed to Christ as her Savior and Lord. Maybe such an argument from silence is unfair; certainly there are many things she has not said. But her affirmation of Christ seems quite essential if her gift of prophecy is to be accepted as God given. Her rejection of Satan means very little. It is hard to find anyone in the occult (except some satanists and a few witches) who doesn't reject Satan. Anton LaVey even denied that he believed in Satan in a *Look* magazine interview. Yet, in his *The Satanic Bible* he writes that Satan is Lord and master, and king of hell.

Mrs. Dixon explains that she knew she was a "worker for the Lord" from the day when, as a child, a gypsy noticed the unusual line patterns in her hand. The gypsy's statement to her about her mission was her "call from God." To her, the call fit in with the prophecy of Joel:

> "And it shall come to pass afterward,
>   that I will pour out my spirit on all flesh;
> your sons and your daughters shall prophesy,
>   your old men shall dream dreams,
>   and your young men shall see visions.
> Even upon the menservants and maidservants
>   in those days, I will pour out my spirit."
>   Joel 2:28-30

Jeane Dixon, famous for her prediction of the slayings of John and Robert Kennedy, has made many predictions that have been completely wrong. But people who go around looking for all of the mistakes and weaknesses in the prophecies of seers, and particularly in the prophecies of Jeane Dixon, should realize that these inconsistencies do not bother her nor those who follow her horoscopes. She says that when a vision is proven to be incorrect, it is not the vision that is wrong, but a wrong interpretation of the symbols. It matters little that she is wrong some of the time. The point is that she is right many times.

People are probably more divided in their feelings about Jeane Dixon than about anyone else in the psychic world. Those who appreciate her call to turn to God, without stressing Jesus Christ, believe that she is a prophetess sent from God.

Others will admit that she has biblical information, but, knowing that Satan has such information as well, are concerned by her call to theism rather than to Christ as Savior. They agree that she is a prophetess, but they wonder who sent her.

Henry Rucker, Director of the Psychic Research Foundation in Chicago, is a sophisticated and fluent black man who preaches reincarnation, astral projection, and clairvoyance in terms that sound almost Christian. He is a persuasive lecturer for Spiritual Frontiers Fellowship and has a way of convincing people of the wonder and attractiveness of the psychic dimensions. One night in Detroit he held teenagers spellbound for three hours as he demonstrated psychic phenomena. Rucker is one of several black spokesmen for the occult.

Lilian Cosby, a clairvoyant, said on National Educational Television's *Black Journal,* "[Clairvoyance] 'was a gift given to me.' " She explained that at age fifteen she predicted an accident on the way to school, and since then she has known and improved her gift of clairvoyance.

According to *Jertha Love,* a black astrologer, blacks are not of Pisces, as many believe, but of Cancer. He said that black people must follow the moon because the moon has sensitivity and psychic powers. To him, the future of the black man is tied in with Cancer.

There are occult leaders everywhere. At any local occult bookstore, there will be people coming and going who have their own small group that they lead or teach. The sales people are teachers as well, willingly answering the questions of the novice. They know the history of the occult and who the various occult leaders are in their community. The underground papers in New York and California advertise the leaders in the occult. They are available for counsel to the troubled and offer answers to any and every problem. The priest or priestess of each coven is also a leader. Leaders are everywhere and people are turning to them. Since there are so many new people every day asking to be taught in the ways of the occult, there will arise still more leaders to teach them.

One point emphasized again and again by leaders of the occult is that theirs is a religion, whether formalized or not. They are seeking the Ultimate Power, Infinite Knowledge, Supreme

Intelligence, or Universal Spirit, and they are serious in their search. Christians wanting to share the liberation in Jesus that they have found in the New Birth should realize that occult believers think of themselves as religious and (in most cases) good people. They do not think of themselves as Satan-owned, but rather as persons looking for a deeper religious life, more power in daily affairs, and harmony with the cosmos. Satan has always appealed to people in this way, and Christians should be alert to his methods. He hasn't changed his tactics; he has fooled people before and he is fooling them now.

"I don't believe in Satan," said a spiritualist minister. She received guidance for her flock from the spirit world. For her, God made it all possible—not Satan.

"I wouldn't be afraid of Satan," said a young witch to a Christian. "He wouldn't hurt me."

And as people in the occult deny the existence of Satan or refer to him as a benevolent spirit, the occult grows, fanned by a force that people call "God" while this force actually keeps people from meeting God.

Whether one stumbles across beheaded chickens around a ritualistic fire in the woods, attends a black mass, or draws the mystic circle with his *athame* (the ritualistic witches' sword), he is drawing on powers beyond himself. These are powers of the world, powers of the demonic, and the powers of a systematic thought that confirms Satan as the god of this world.

7
The God of This World

"There were thirteen of us behind the house. It was dark except for the small fire burning. It was the night we planned to conjure up Satan. And, it worked! When he appeared, he was green and black, with both hands held up in front of him like a surgeon who has washed up. I knew it was Satan and I became so frightened that I left and never went back."

Those are the words of a young Christian who went through drugs, witchcraft, and finally the worship of Satan before he came to the point where his involvement with Satan frightened him so much that he turned in terror to Jesus Christ to be freed. The occurrences of meeting Satan are becoming more frequent, but they don't affect everybody the same way. A young woman who also saw Satan in a black arts ceremony had the opposite reaction. She went out and stabbed a sixty-two-year-old man to death. She told a *Newsweek* reporter, August 16, 1971, "I even had an orgasm while stabbing him."

What begins as simply a desire to experiment with the occult or to search for power draws a person until he is no longer dabbling in the occult; the occult possesses him.

Dr. James D. Lisle, a Norwalk, California, psychologist, said in a Ridder News Service interview, "You can never be sure a person involved in this won't step over the line into infant sacrifice or cannibalism. We have evidence that it happens." *(St. Paul Dispatch,* June 8, 1972). The same article proves Lisle's point with the reminder that in July, 1970, "the torso of a social worker was found floating in Yellowstone River with the heart carved out."

The occult, regardless of direction or how bizarre it becomes, is basically a religious quest coming out of the emptiness inside of people. Man longs for a contact with the beyond, whether he calls it "god" or "force." He knows that there are powers outside of himself. He has felt the lack in his own life caused by a starved soul, and he has seen the results of these larger forces in the lives of others. This combination of emptiness and desire send him searching in the occult for what he lacks.

When witches form a circle to keep out hostile forces and through chanting and dancing they worship the powers that "be," they are not just acting out a prelude to an orgy. They are seeking access to the radiation or powers that emanate from mother earth, from the stars and moon, and from each other. If a visitor looking for excitement tries to come into the group, the witches will firmly ask him to leave. They are committed to an experience that cannot be broken by curious onlookers. Even though there are always a few faddists who are "into witchcraft" for fun and will invite the press in to take pictures, most covens won't let reporters in unless they are willing to enter into the celebration with a proper attitude of worship.

Most covens do not seek new members either. Rituals are usually held secretly to discourage visitors. A person who wants to get into a coven must first seek out other witches, learn the religious ritual of witchcraft from them, and prove that he is committed to being a witch.

When satanists pray their prayers for destruction or lust, or respond to the priest's word "Shemhamforash" with "Hail, Satan," they are not simply having a good time. They are seriously mocking God and calling upon the powers of their god. Satan does answer the prayers of people who are yielded to him. Satan has power to give, and in return for that power his followers try to keep their loyalty pure. It is their religion.

A student doing a research paper on satanism tried for two years to join a satanist church. He was not allowed to join because the worshipers knew that his motives did not include the desire to worship Satan. When two students from a Christian college in California tried to visit a satanist church, the officiating priest announced that he could not go on because there were people present who were not there to worship Satan. Even though he did not know who they were, he could tell by the block in the worship experience that someone was not in sympathy with what they were doing. The students had to leave.

The worship of Satan through pacts and prayers and rituals is, for most people, an attempt to be honest. The people in satanism want to practice what they preach. Anton LaVey has expressed his conviction that the greatest contributors to the rise of satanism have been the Christians. He sees Christians as unnatural, holding back their real feelings. To LaVey, the Christian church functions by hypocrisy. So he created a church where the black arts, lust, and power-seeking are virtues, and people can be what LaVey says they really are. Apparently he is right; satanism is appealing to thousands.

When people heed their horoscopes or have astrological charts especially drawn to help them guide their lives, they point to evidence that these attempts do work. Astrological guidance is not just self-suggestion. When people sense the emanations or vibrations from everything around them, and line up with the forces of the stars, the moon, and the sun, they feel a smoothness and harmony in life that makes them firm believers and strong proclaimers of their religion. They are not just pretending that they have found a source of order.

Everything in the universe, according to believers in astrology, is orderly. Its patterns and rhythms are attractive because most people's lives are chaotic. They don't know which way to turn or what decisions to make or why "everything seems to happen to me." To believers in astrology, coming into harmony with the smoothness of the universal order is like coming into harmony with God. For them this relationship is wonderful. They become quieter, more peaceful, better-balanced individuals. Their energies are not drained off in frustrated running this way and that. They have a sense of destiny and purpose. They are better organized in their daily living.

When followers of astrology apply their discoveries to the people around them, they find that they are building better human relations. One person doesn't antagonize another whom he knows is in an astrologically difficult time of life. He bends more and tries not to make that person's life any harder than it already is. He has discovered from the charts that certain astrological conjunctions have come together for that person so that he is going to have a rough time until he works out of it. The follower of astrology assists and helps and visits or does not visit certain people on certain days. In other words, he has an expanded awareness of where other people are, and he helps them with their needs. He is not following some form of superstition; he is religiously trying to be a better man.

"Oh, now wait a minute, aren't we taking all of this occult business just a little too seriously?" questions a man who reads the popular news magazine articles about some of the bizarre behavior of people in the occult. "It's just fun. There may be a few fanatics who have killed people, but most people in the occult aren't serious. They don't really guide their lives by the stars; everyone looks at his horoscope occasionally. And they don't really trust the tarot cards or Ouija boards. It's just curiosity. It may be a superstition, like carrying a rabbit's foot, but it certainly isn't a religion!"

Such conclusions are easily reached. The "fun" of the occult makes interesting reading, and reporters know it. And most of the people who allow their pictures to be taken by a national news magazine are just having a good time. The occult is like a party, sort of a holiday fling, a type of relaxation—at least that's what comes across to the person who reads about nude dancing, seances, and Pan Am's $629 "Psychic Tour" of occult places in Great Britain.

But when a reporter looks beneath the surface trappings and enters into quiet conversation with the serious occult believer, he gets an entirely different picture. The craving for ritual and power beyond oneself, for honesty and a contact with the greater forces are all expressions of a religious need. Between this need and the answers offered in the revelations of God, Satan enters to give quasi-answers. He offers more power, more satisfaction, more security and harmony with the world than a person can get by his own abilities. He satisfies people with more than they could ever have in themselves but with far less than God offers in the peace, harmony, and completing wholeness in Christ Jesus. As a result, believers in the occult are sincere believers in the best that they know. They have been blinded by the god of this world, have missed Christ, but they go through life rejoicing that they have more than they have ever had before.

They are genuine, sincere, and, perhaps far more than many Christian church members, committed to what they are doing.

They try to mature in their faith, and they bear witness about their discoveries to their friends. They are eager to share the happy life that they have discovered. They teach one another and pray for one another, and many groups have a genuine sense of brotherhood. In witchcraft, whole covens will concentrate their energies on a member who has some need. They care about each other. People have been healed, problems have been solved, and one coven claims 100 percent success in casting preventative spells for young men who want to avoid the draft.

Satan satisfies. He duplicates most of the Christian gifts, offers a dimension and depth of meaning to human existence that gives satisfaction, even if only temporarily, and he enslaves. *The International Standard Bible Encyclopedia* summarizes what happens when a person goes to Satan for answers and fulfillment: "The agent of Satan is always a victim." [1]

"That's a lie," protests the person who prides himself in his willingness to accept people's differences. "They may disagree with mainline religious thinking, but that doesn't mean that persons who practice clairvoyant gifts, or read Jeane Dixon in their newspapers, are servants of Satan."

To the casual observer of the occult, or the person involved in occult practices with the sincere purpose of "serving God," the charge of "Satan-owned" seems very harsh.

A mother said, "We cast a spell for the healing of our child and our child was healed. Are you trying to say that Satan did that?"

A witch added. "There is nothing wrong with a little white witchcraft. I wouldn't worship Satan."

"I agree," says another. "I made a love potion and gave it to the man of my dreams and now we are happily married. Don't tell me that God didn't work that out for us. Our happiness proves that he did."

A spiritualist testified, "When someone I loved very much died, I was in agony until a medium assured me that I would see my loved one again. I can't tell you the peace I now feel. God blessed me by sending me to that medium."

The ministers of the occult churches, professional mediums, and astrologers do not use their powers or gifts for themselves, explains a psychic. If they did, they would lose them. They give of

---

[1] *The International Standard Bible Encyclopedia* (Chicago: The Howard-Severance Company, 1915), vol. 4, p. 2694.

themselves, offering their services to their fellowman. They charge only so that they can live, too. They plead that surely such dedication can't be Satanic.

"You certainly cannot call such things as astrology a work of Satan," says a Christian pastor. He described a parishioner whose whole life has been improved and blessed because her marriage has been mended through astrology.

"She is a committed, born-again Christian," he states. "She has accepted Jesus Christ as her Savior and I baptized her."

He explained that she was having marital problems, but through astrology she came to understand why her husband acted as he did and why she behaved certain ways. She has learned through astrology how to anticipate his bad days by knowing his horoscope, and she reacts accordingly. She also anticipates her own bad days and avoids stress and conflict on those days. As a result, harmony has come into their married life, and she thanks God for it. God brought her the help she needed through astrology, she says.

"She is devoted to God, because of astrology," claims her pastor. "Astrology was the healing factor. It is like any other form of medication or therapy, and you can't call medication and therapy Satanic."

Satan is very subtle. He can and will offer anything. It doesn't bother him if people think he is God. Satan will even encourage persons to serve God as long as they follow his own ways in doing so. All the time praising God, this Christian who practiced astrology was gravitating toward occult means to receive the help that God longs to give. God can heal a broken marriage and bind two people together much more completely than Satan can. God made the two people; he knows them best and can fill them with something that Satan can't give, God's love. Yet she chose another way, while all the time insisting it was God's way.

"Could it have been God's way?" some ask. "Maybe the woman is right."

If it is God's way, why does he so often in Scripture warn people away from it? God loves his people too much and knows the ways of Satan too well. The warnings are there, but a person must want to heed them.

Time usually reveals who really controls a person. When Satan begins to get hold of persons, he will make sure that they get what they want. Then slowly he weans them away from trusting in God for the answers to their needs. Unfortunately, those who turn from God to Satan don't usually know that they are drifting until they are so completely entrenched with Satan that a radical form of spiritual exorcism is necessary to set them free. Sometimes, even when the work of Satan is pointed out to them, they think that what they are looking at is the work of God.

A young woman in Denver is a good example. She shared her experiences with a Christian.

"My great-great-grandmother came into the party, sat down, and we had an intelligent conversation. Others at the party noticed her and asked, 'Who is that?' It was really tremendous. I had never met my great-great-grandmother before. She's been dead since long before I was born.

"But I knew it was she, and she has since returned many times to talk to me. When things are going badly, she comes. She has been a real help to me. She is young, like a college girl, but very, very wise. Sometimes I feel her presence when I go into a trance. I've had the same kind of contact with my grandfather on my father's side. You see, I'm a psychic. It makes me perceptive."

"But aren't you afraid that this will possess you? Do you believe in a Satanic power?"

"No, I can't really believe in a Satanic power. I don't cast spells like the witches. I don't believe in that sort of thing. If I did something harmful with a spell, it would come back to me twofold—I just know that. I'm very conscious of God and Jesus. They are very definitely there."

"Do you ever pray, asking God to help you with your needs?"

"I wanted to reach out to Jesus one time, but nothing was there. So I started screaming, 'I need you,' and my great-great-grandmother came. She's like a messenger from God. God was too busy; so she came. Maybe he didn't feel the need to help me since my great-great-grandmother and I communicate so well.

"I think about the hereafter and talk about it with her. She said I would join her when I drop my body—and I will join her. I don't know where, but with Jesus. I believe in Jesus as Savior. I was baptized as a born-again believer in a Baptist church, but when I need help, it's my great-great-grandmother who comes, not Jesus."

"Then you believe in God?"

"Well, he's more of a controlling presence. He's larger than that. 'God' is too narrow."

"Do you believe in Satan?"

"I don't know if I acknowledge the presence of Satan. Evil and good are in man; they just sort of peek through. We can overcome it in ourselves. Everything has to come from within yourself."

"Well, then, is God your own creation?"

"Probably so. I think something has created man, and man has created God for his own comfort. A 'Presence' created man."

"How do you handle the words of Jesus, 'I am the way, and the truth, and the life; no one comes to the Father, but by me'?"

"Well, that's a matter of interpretation. The ideas he is teaching will save man, not the man Jesus himself. If man is going to survive, he has need of Jesus' teaching, but I don't go along with the Son of God thing. There are many Messiahs—Buddha, Mehir Baba, and others. Man has to save himself."

"Then you don't feel a need for God personally?"

"Everybody does, yes. I need God. I've got it [sic]. Whatever I need to know will be planted there in me."

"You said that you were a baptized believer in a church. Do you go to church?"

"No, that's very interesting. God doesn't want me in church anymore. You see the last time I went to church I was really concentrating on the message. When somebody is trying to tell me something, I try to analyze it, saying to myself, 'OK, what is he trying to tell you? Think it out. What's he saying?' So I was concentrating on the sermon and for no biological reason I fainted. The next thing I knew, I was outside and an ambulance was there. That was God's way of telling me that I didn't need the rules and the regulations of the church anymore."

"Let me suggest another reason that you might have fainted. If I were Satan, and you were concentrating on a message that might have convinced you that Jesus Christ really is God and Savior, I think I would have done the same thing to you. Satan blocked the message. Did you ever think of that?"

"Well, if this was Satan, he would be having me do bad things. I don't do bad things."

"I don't think so. If Satan had you doing bad things, it would be repugnant to you and you would turn away from him. But he will have you do good things on his terms. He is disguised as an angel of light; what he does and encourages you to do can be very good. Why would he tempt you to do evil, if by doing good through his power, he can keep you from an understanding and a commitment to Jesus Christ?"

"I guess I never thought of that."

It is hard for people to understand the work of Satan. As the god of this world, he doesn't have to drag people into evil. Satan will keep good people doing good things if it will keep them from recognizing and responding to Jesus. The apostle Paul summarized it: ". . . the god of this world has blinded the minds of the unbelievers, to keep them from seeing the light of the gospel of the glory of Christ, who is the likeness of God" (2 Corinthians 4:4).

The grip of Satan is very strong. While strengthening his hold on an individual, he calls what he is doing the work of God. The one possessed by Satan is not necessarily evil in his thoughts or actions, nor does he understand that he is possessed. He thinks that he is free, freer than the Christian. And in his "freedom" he avoids the outreaching love of God shown to him in the coming of Jesus Christ. Instead he keeps on striving and searching and pleading for some still greater mystical experience that will seem godly and satisfy him temporarily.

No matter how hard occult people try to find God, they never are given the assurance that they have found him. Satan can counterfeit many things, but he cannot counterfeit Christian assurance. Even if they believe in reincarnation, with many chances to improve themselves and a never-ending series of lifetimes moving upward to higher and higher planes, they never find God. When the series finally ends, the best that they can hope for is to reach a plane where God once was. The experience is the same in all of the other branches of the occult. People commit themselves more and more to the power that is greater than themselves, finding some answers but only enough to keep them searching.

The deeper peace, the knowledge of being reborn and totally alive, is never discovered by the follower of the occult. He protests to the Christian that the way of Christ is too narrow. He will insist that there are many ways to God and explains that Jesus is only one way. That's all he can do with Jesus. If he ever admitted that what Jesus said about himself is true, then he would have to face him honestly. But as long as he can convince himself that Jesus is one of many ways, then he can make Jesus into anything he wants him to be. He can quote the teachings of Jesus his own way, or he can make Jesus a fellow struggler or an example on his terms.

Occult people will hedge about Jesus or explain him away if they can, but if forced to make a decision about whether he is the saving Son of God who loves them, they will usually deny him. Satan keeps his people from a direct encounter with Jesus as long as he can. He tries to satisfy their religious quest himself. But if they have to decide about Christ and there is no way to sidestep, he will tell them to say, "No!"

Some people are coming to Jesus Christ out of the occult, but they have faced great difficulty in doing so. They have to be really aware and even frightened of what possesses them. Even then, some can't pry themselves away from what little security or power they have in Satan to trust Christ for liberation. One man, who knowingly once made a blood pact with Satan, listened with tears in his eyes to the offer of freedom and salvation through Jesus Christ. But to the offer "Why don't you let Jesus Christ free you from this pact with Satan and give you new life?" he responded: "I want to, but I can't."

Christians are beginning to see what Satanic possession is. It is rooted in the deep religious need of man to find peace and harmony and security and a reason for being. Satan has convinced people to look in other "superior, more mystical" directions for what God wants to give. He keeps them where they "will listen to anybody and can never arrive at a knowledge of the truth" (2 Timothy 3:7). This occult possession has a narrowing quality about it because it limits the vision more and more as the occult seeker searches more desperately yet is locked in tighter the farther he goes. As if in a tunnel, the "light" attracts him, but he can't see the wider view.

The Christian who is committed, not simply to an institution or cultural Christianity but to the living, reigning Christ, feels a tremendous burden in his heart for these people. He yearns for the deliverance of those whose hearts have been captured by the god of this earth. The sensitive Christian is awed by the confusing, blinding power of this demonic force. He does not deny that "all have sinned and fall short of the glory of God" (Romans 3:23), but understands that there is a demonic ownership that is based on a seeking after demonized forces. This goes far deeper than the Satanic ownership of all who are still dead in sin.

Christians, alert to Satan and his power, are also alert to the "cosmic" wholeness offered to men by the Redeemer who long ago announced, "I saw Satan fall like lightning. . . ."

8 "I Saw Satan Fall like Lightning from Heaven"

Jesus spoke quite candidly about Satan. His followers need to do the same. But not every disciple is prepared to do it.

For example, one person protested, "Oh, come on, what real proof is there that this occult stuff works? Is there anything more conclusive than what they say?" No matter how much evidence was shown to him, this Christian only sat back and said, "Well, that certainly isn't conclusive."

Others have become so frightened of the reports that they hear that they have closed their eyes and fallen into a self-induced coma, apparently with the hope that somehow all of "that nasty occult business" will go away. One Christian expressed the feelings of many others: "I don't even want to talk about it; it's too frightening."

A few have determined theologically that there isn't even an issue to be discussed as Christians. When confronted with the beliefs of the satanists, one pastor exclaimed, "Why do they speak so reverently of Satan? The church long ago outgrew the idea of a personal real Devil!"

Satan is real. Jesus spoke about him and what he is trying to do in the world. The followers of Jesus need to hear their Master and take him seriously. A person is quite presumptuous to say, "I'm a follower of Jesus, but I don't agree with everything that he says." Nor does it help much to add the qualifier, "Well, I agree with Jesus, but I have a different interpretation of what he meant."

Satan is real, too, for the many who draw their power from him.

And although many occult people will use some name other than "Satan" or explain the Devil as a benevolent, not an evil, force, they have committed their lives to that force. Yet there are still Christians who do not believe that there are demonic forces and who will not take occult people seriously when they try to explain their own religious convictions.

The Scriptures refer to Satan as a slanderer, an accuser, an adversary, a prowling lion seeking to devour, and the one disguised as an angel of light. Christians who dismiss Satan as a silly idea, or a concept taught by the immature, or who explain evil merely as the absence of good, are ignoring the key to Satan's sly power. He does deceive people, both believers and unbelievers. He has a reason for wanting to do it. Kent Philpott, who encountered the occult in his work in Haight-Ashbury, told *Home Missions* magazine (January, 1972), "Basically, God loves us and the devil, very simply, opposes God, and wants to destroy what God loves."

Satan knows who God is and understands very well the significance of the wholeness that redemption brings to man. When he counterfeits the gospel, he can make his teachings and the teachings of God sound very much alike. He has the power to confuse man. One person, in trying to describe the nature and influence of Satan, said, "He is the fourth person, just below the Trinity but far superior to man."

It should not be surprising then that Satan knows how to twist God's truth. He understands it with a comprehension that far exceeds man's own theology. Even revelation is God's truth put on terms that man understands. Satan can grasp far more than that. When he corrupts the gospel, he corrupts from a position of great comprehension.

Satan can teach that eternal life is really a "life force" that continues on after death, and it sounds very plausible. He tells those who will listen to him that Jesus' purpose in talking about eternal life was to give us a higher view of the afterlife. To people who like "deeper truth," this kind of teaching is heady stuff.

Satan is able to take "new birth" and twist it to mean "new life," which means, in his definition, an ever-emerging life that is always newer than it was. He teaches an ongoing life-expanding experience that takes a progressing person sometimes into the spirit world and sometimes into the physical experience of our world, and always calls it the work of God.

He is able to make prayer sound like telepathy and telepathy sound like prayer. An encounter with a consciousness beyond our own, or an encounter with the spirit world, becomes a warm, glowing experience. Why, he suggests, should we just contact a nebulous concept like "God" when there are exciting people to talk to on "the other side" whose many experiences can offer us counsel and advice?

Satan teaches, through reincarnation, that there is no "emergency" about sin and salvation. We are all going to have many lifetimes to improve ourselves. God planned it that way so that we could become more and more like him. Also, appealing to man's "do-it-yourself" feelings, he emphasizes reincarnation's opportunities for carrying on or improving projects begun on earth. That offer of additional lifetimes makes the gift of eternal life seem almost bland.

When people begin to wonder if the statements of Scripture just might be true, Satan offers them the "larger" understanding of visions and dream revelations. Is it possible that "God spoke of old to our fathers by the prophets"? It really doesn't matter, says Satan. They were inspired, but so are we in our dream revelations from God which are much more meaningful and current. We can ignore the old revelations of ancient prophets if we have the new revelation of last night's dream.

The reality of satanism and demonic forces in the modern occult renaissance requires that the Christian be alert to Satan and knowledgeable about his ways. But he doesn't have to panic. Every Christian could learn from the elderly member of one church who announced, "I'm not afraid of Satan." She explained that she has committed herself in trust to Jesus Christ who has already secured the final victory over Satan.

This elderly lady went on to admit that she respected the power of Satan. She wasn't ignoring him. She had seen enough in her lifetime to know that there is a Satanic force, not just a psychological need in man to be "secretive" or "naughty."

The alert Christian separates the "fun" of the occult from "life surrender" to it. He does not lump all occult practices together. There have always been "black arts" groups throughout history who have really been thrill seekers. And some so-called satanist groups are, in fact, just thinly disguised sex clubs. There are many people who only "fool around" with horoscopes and mediums and

Ouija boards. The Christian knows that, although he also sees the subtle influence of Satan there, too.

But the Christian also recognizes dedication. People are building their whole life-style on the direction of astrology charts. They are struggling with mind science as a way to God. They are reading the tarot cards and listening to the spirits and exploring the world of clairvoyance, telepathy, and astral projection. And if they can find some meaning to life, they are willing to turn themselves over to Satan.

Victor H. Ernest, in his book *I Talked with Spirits*, tells of two people who worshiped Satan on the banks of the Mississippi. Prostrating themselves, they prayed to be chosen to take the anti-Christ to the world.[1]

The alert Christian notes all of this that is happening, and he is discerning. He is prepared to heed Paul's exhortation:

> Be strong in the Lord and in the strength of his might. Put on the whole armor of God, that you may be able to stand against the wiles of the devil. For we are not contending against flesh and blood, but against the principalities, against the powers, against the world rulers of this present darkness, against the spiritual hosts of wickedness in the heavenly places. Therefore take the whole armor of God, that you may be able to withstand in the evil day, and having done all, to stand (Ephesians 6:10-13).

And he is concerned enough for people to want them to have the life-giving fullness that God offers men in Christ Jesus.

These are apocalyptic times. Aquarians and Christians know it. While psychics predict the coming of a new world with the decline of Christianity and the ushering in of a glorious age of Aquarian love, hundreds of thousands of others, particularly street people, are turning in faith to Jesus Christ. These Christians, coming out of the dark tunnel that included trips into the occult, are also anticipating a new age and a new leader, all tied together in Christ's return.

The pressure of Satan's campaign for men cannot be casually dismissed. During these days people are gravitating to Satan and the occult because they are spiritually in need. They cannot be condemned nor blamed for it. God made all men with souls that are restless until filled with himself. The longing is natural, and to

[1] Victor H. Ernest, *I Talked with Spirits* (Wheaton, Ill.; Tyndale House Publishers, 1971), p. 60.

those blinded to the offer of God, Satan's substitutes are attractive. They have to have something. God, knowing the need of man, has made his offer of life, fulfillment, and peace. Christians who really love people cannot keep silent about that offer.

The revival of the occult is beginning to waken Christians to the reality of the activity of Satan. There has been an assumption, apparently by many, that people either had Jesus Christ or they didn't have Jesus Christ. Now it is becoming clear that not to have Jesus is not a neutral position; it is a position of enslavement because man cannot exist in a spiritual vacuum. He will either have Christ or Satan, but he will not have an empty soul.

Christians who have been taking up their time with sanctified busyness, concentrating on peripheral church matters, and letting Satan have the fields that are white unto harvest, have to rethink their priorities. Those who have been enjoying the luxury of arguing with each other over minor theological points or denominational differences can't afford that luxury any longer. And Christians who have been yawning their way through an ordinary, mediocre Christian life, neither doing or becoming for Christ, can't be that way anymore. Christians have work to do.

When believers experience the fullness of the "depths of the riches and wisdom and knowledge" of God in Christ, they will no longer be too busy, too lazy, too narrow, or too shocked at what Satan is doing in the world. Instead, they will respond to the commissioning of Jesus, and their mission in Jesus' name will start producing results.

Scripture is supportive of Christian believers. "The reason the Son of God appeared was to destroy the works of the devil" (1 John 3:8). So, to hold onto the Son is to hold onto a victory over Satan that is already in God's hand. Scripture further confirms that the believer is already delivered ". . . from the dominion of darkness," and already transferred to "the kingdom of his beloved Son" (Colossians 1:13). And he knows that "If the Son makes you free, you will be free indeed" (John 8:36).

The Christian has two responsibilities. He must stay with Christ, living in him; he must help others to find the freedom that they need now in Jesus.

LIVING IN CHRIST

A young Christian, writing from a Jesus commune in New York, said, "Satan will continue to blind, confuse, and counterfeit all that God has in store for people. His main battle with Christians is to render them ineffective for the Lord Jesus Christ and cause hurt or shame to his name. The Devil has had some degree of success in confusing people about his own reality."

Life in Christ does not exempt a person from Satan's attempts to influence his life. Being in Christ, having been transferred into the kingdom of light, a believer has an awareness of Satan that the person outside of the light of Christ doesn't have. He sees the influence that others do not see. He knows that Satan is working in the world, including himself. The Christian who does not have a sense of Satan could be in danger of either not having responded to Christ, thus not knowing the contrast between darkness and light, or else he has already been seduced by Satan without having even been aware that he was propositioned.

Satan will draw the Christian into his way if he can. Christians who experiment with the occult soon find themselves becoming spiritually cold, praying less or not at all, beginning to avoid the assembly of believers and losing their sensitive Christian concerns for the world around them. It has happened many times. One man experienced the attacks of Satan just from his "objective" study of the occult.

Christians must consciously stay within the clarity of the gospel and the relationship that they have in Christ. Those who do undertake this deliberate step are assured by the promise: "Resist the devil and he will flee from you" (James 4:7). The Christian must always remember to whom he belongs and whom he serves. The drift toward the occult can start very easily. God knows that and early in the Scriptures he purposely warned: "Do not turn to mediums or wizards; do not seek them out, to be defiled by them: I am the Lord your God" (Leviticus 19:31).

A fairly new Christian, seeking the power of prayer, soon found himself thinking of prayer as magic. He prayed for God to work certain ways, to give him particular spiritual gifts. Soon he was a prayer manipulator rather than a yielded person. When he got his eyes on the end rather than the means, he began to drift into magic. He found that it was all the same to him to pray for something or to cast a spell for something. Not much time is needed for Satan to confuse a weak Christian.

The church is partially to blame for some of the drift toward the occult. As organized religion has grown sterile and cold, people have turned elsewhere for the satisfaction of their mystical longings. Right at the time in history when people are looking for new dimensions of understanding themselves, a contact with powers that are beyond, and a relationship to the supernatural, many Christians have explained God in the cold, test-tube terms that scientism has used to explain its religion. There has been expressed a deep yearning by man for a harmony with the cosmos and an experience with the unseen forces. Yet Christian explanations of God have often stripped him of his transcendence and indescribable power.

The tremendous mystery of God has been played down, overorganized, or sterilized by so many Christian witnesses that the soul seeking the supernatural God is left aching and void. In an eagerness to point out the Counselor, Friend, and other in-carnational aspects of God, the total "otherness" of God has been minimized. So modern man, empty from his overexposure to the rational and the scientific, and longing for the supernatural that his soul and his senses tell him is out there someplace, turns to the occult religions. And the occult lures him with the promise of experiencing not the limited, small brother God of the Christians, but the Divine Intelligence, the Universal Spirit, the First Cause, the Ultimate Power, the Infinite Presence. In short, the occult has the seeds of the old first-century gnosticism which has surfaced many times in church history. This heresy has taken many forms, but always it promises to satisfy man's "larger" or "deeper" religious needs.

The occult is more than man trying to reach up to God while ignoring the fact that God is reaching down to man. It is a seeking after greater revelation and greater "God concepts" than Judeo-Christian teaching offers. The Gnostic and the occultist claim that the "real" God is beyond and larger than the God that is taught by the church. They say that Jesus is too small; he is "a" way but not "the" way. There are greater supernatural mysteries to be discovered, revelations from the spirits, directions from the cosmic order, progressions to be made to higher and higher planes, and forces to be experienced that enhance man's ESP and "psi."

If we look under the occult, we will discover the ancient Gnostic heresies that have always tried to subvert the Christian doctrine of God. If modern occult gnosticism is not exactly like first-century gnosticism, it is very close—even closer than some of the branches of gnosticism that have plagued the church in other centuries. Angelic beings, direct revelations, mysteries from the eternal spirit, Jesus taught to be less than God, the denial of the flesh that in reality indulges the flesh, and the staircase theology that has man moving up through the various emanations of deity are descriptive of the occult offerings.

Man needs the fullness of God in Christ, and he is seeking it now. The earthly ministry of Jesus is not limited, nor is his incarnation minimized by the powerful assertion of John:

> In the beginning was the Word, and the Word was with God, and the Word was God. He was in the beginning with God; all things were made through him, and without him was not anything made that was made (John 1:1-3).

Man needs to hear that again. He also needs to hear that when he reaches out to the "larger" God by human wisdom, or the revelation of angels or spirits, he is seeking God by means that Jesus Christ as the fullness of God has already "led captive." Like a conqueror who has returned from the battle with his conquered train behind him, "He [Jesus] disarmed the principalities and powers and made a public example of them triumphing over them in him" (Colossians 2:15). These so-called higher principalities and powers that are attractive to the occult have failed to provide any kind of pathway to God and have long ago been shown to be part of the victory procession of the cosmic Christ who is God.

To proclaim Jesus Christ is to proclaim more than a teacher, healer, and friend. He is that, but not just that:

> He is the image of the invisible God, the first-born of all creation; for in him all things were created, in heaven and on earth, visible and invisible, whether thrones or dominions or principalities or authorities—all things were created through him and for him. He is before all things, and in him all things hold together. He is the head of the body, the church; he is the beginning, the first-born from the dead, that in everything he might be pre-eminent. For in him all the fulness of God was pleased to dwell, and through him to reconcile to himself all things, whether on earth or in heaven, making peace by the blood of his cross (Colossians 1:15-20).

Because of this cosmic nature of Jesus, Christians can also teach the desperately searching occult believer that he can know God and be reconciled to God through this One:

who, though he was in the form of God, did not count equality with God a thing to be grasped, but emptied himself, taking the form of a servant, being born in the likeness of men. And being found in human form he humbled himself and became obedient unto death, even death on a cross (Philippians 2:6-8).

The Scriptures teach the balance of the "totally other God" *and* the fullness of God in the man Christ Jesus. The mystical, combined with the personal encounter, sought after by the occult people who practice a form of modern-day gnosticism, is offered in the Christian message if Christians will present it. This message neither excludes the transcendent awesomeness of God, nor rejects the totally human incarnate God. There is a mystery about God and about life, but if men do not find the answers to that great mystery in Christ, they will look for it in Gnostic occultism.

Some Christians, who know that they need to present the whole Christ, are going to have to make some adjustments in their christological concepts. At the one extreme, Christians who stress Jesus only, in sort of a Jesus Unitarianism, are going to have to realize that they are talking about *God*. The syrupy love ballads sung to Jesus and the arm around the shoulder buddy relationship will repel the man who knows that God is omnipotent and omnipresent and can't be approached that way. The occult offers him a mysterious god, and he will soon be caught up in the great deception of Satan, pushed in that direction by an unbalanced Christian theology.

On the other hand, there is the opposite extreme of some Christians who put so much stress on the otherness of God that he is presented as unapproachable in his holiness and too majestic to ever be concerned about our personal aches and pains. These Christians obscure the great message of God in Christ reconciling the world to himself. They do not teach that Jesus was born, grew up, was tempted as we are, and knows every hair on our heads. They forget that God is "Our Father" in an intimacy that cannot be matched by any human relationship, and that he calls us to himself. This one-sided Christian presentation will also drive away the man who is looking for an encounter with the Divine that is personal and real and warm. The occult can offer him a god that is so personally concerned for him that he blends him into the whole structure of the universal order. Satan can make him feel like he is intimately one with the cosmos and that all of the "good" forces are being released into his life through the love of God.

The International Standard Bible Encyclopedia refers to "the balance and sanity of the Bible" as the answer for the offerings of Satan.[2] When Christians stick to the whole message of the Bible, they will have adequate food for their souls and will find the deep message of God that occult people seek.

Living in Christ offers a dimension of worship and fellowship that occult people are seeking, too. When Christ established his church, it was to be a community of power-filled, loving, caring, spirit-led people whose lives and worship would glorify God. The church is potentially a great community. Yet somehow, people searching for community are finding the companionship of a coven or the brotherhood of spirits before they are finding the fellowship of the church. They are responding to the ritual of satanism and the prayers before a seance instead of discovering the magnificence of Christian praise and worship.

Without taking anything away from the blinding influence of Satan, who certainly doesn't want people to see what Jesus Christ offers, some of the blame must be placed on the church. David Bubar, an ex-minister who now holds seances and uses his powers to guide the profit making of seventeen corporations, explained that people can find spiritual things outside of the church. *Home Missions* magazine (January, 1972) quoted Bubar who said, "Christ's church died in about 300 A.D. when it ceased to deal with spiritual matters and man began to build his own contraption which he called 'church.' "

Bubar may be extreme in his statements, but many Christians and their churches have blocked the warmth and blessedness of God's pervasive Spirit and have lost the awesome quality of meaningful worship. Because of this lack, many churches are saying loud and clear to the occult seeker, "We don't have anything here either."

Man has a need for the warmth of family feeling that is so much a part of the real church. Honesty, genuine praying for one another, counseling a Christian brother who needs help, and just being responsive to people as valuable, precious persons is what the fellowship of believers is all about. We need each other. There is little family feeling in passing a covered dish on Wednesday night to a person whom you know only by his name tag. Any occult group

---

[2] *The International Standard Bible Encyclopedia* (Chicago: The Howard-Severance Company, 1915), vol. 4, p. 2694.

can offer more than that. But the occult cannot offer the "you are important to me" feeling that is quite uniquely Christian. That feeling comes only with the security of knowing who we are, to whom we belong, and where we are going, and it liberates us to risk ourselves for others even if they reject us. Satan can offer more human interest than the world as a whole can offer, but he can't offer genuine Christian love; the church can—and must.

Another need of man will be met by the worship offered by the balanced church. Dissatisfied Christians, and others who yearn to stand in the presence of God, do not always find real worship in some Christian assemblies. The cacophony of noise that suddenly stops with the call to worship which says, "The program is about to begin," doesn't say, "Surely God is in this place." The "hymns of praise" that are simply mouthed without thought given to the meaning are neither hymns nor praise. And the Lord's Prayer, given by Jesus so that his followers wouldn't "heap up empty phrases" like the heathen do, is often just that—heaped up empty phrases repeated like prayers of the heathen.

There is ritual and awe in the occult. Their gods are respected as gods. The people gather with purpose, dedicate themselves consciously, and know who their god is because they have pushed everything else aside to honor him with singleness of heart. But the occult can't offer the response from God, the reassurance that he hears us and is closer than hands and feet. The church, the Bride of Christ, has this awareness of God and should not hide it. In the awe and reverence of encountering the Infinite God in the human dimension lies the mystery of the church. It satisfies, for God is the Great Satisfaction. The occult cannot match that.

The lack in the spiritual lives of so many Christians, the failure to lay claim to the riches available in Christ Jesus, has pointed many people toward the occult where they can find what they need. The occult is attractive. Not just curiosity leads people to try the Ouija board, visit a medium, study their horoscopes, or join a coven. They do so with an eagerness for the added dimensions found in psychic living. They are looking for the very dimensions that the church already has to offer.

The mental anguish and spiritual pain that people in the occult will endure just to have what Christians have ought to make every Christian weep.

"Spiritualists who want guidance know that they are close to demon possession," said an ex-spiritualist. "We always made the sign of the cross to avoid contact with demon spirits."

To want the kind of guidance that God offers through his Holy Spirit so much that they will risk demon possession to get it is truly frightening. Christians need to know what such people are going through, and they need to care!

Satan understands the longing of the human soul and knows how to use that longing for his own advantage. "The Devil will give anything," said a man who was once a part of the occult. "He will satisfy a person's wants, before he takes."

Somebody else explained, "If a person will surrender to the power of Satan, Satan will give him real power, but he will also own that person."

The Christian can understand that. Christians have always taught that a believer surrenders to Christ, becoming as a slave. He doesn't drift into commitment, but rather gathers up all that he is, and all that he ever hopes to be, and lays it at the feet of Christ. In so doing he opens himself up to the completion, fulfillment, empowering and indwelling of Jesus. He does it willingly, knowing the meaning of discipleship.

The same process is followed in the occult. Whether a person turns directly to Satan or to the god that Satan points him to, he is looking to a power other than the living God to satisfy his life. He has to surrender to that power if it is going to "help" him. For example, the tarot won't work if the person looking for guidance isn't willing to follow the guidance without reservation. Spirits won't help if a person isn't committed to obeying them. And Satan won't empower until a person is drawn into obedience to that power.

If a person thinks that he can have Christ on his own terms, he is deceived. If he thinks that he can have Satan on his own terms, he is also deceived. Discipleship has the same requirements, regardless of whom we serve. The difference is that Christ offers love, protection, and upbuilding to make us totally alive. Satan offers hate and destruction and keeps us from ever obtaining life.

Understanding Satan, and what he is doing through the revival of the occult, adds new meaning to "living in Christ." It is no longer enough to just know about him, or even to live near him. The meaning of "Christ-one," especially when Satan is becoming so powerful, is to live *in* him.

Living in Christ means consciously building one another up in the faith. Christians are responsible to strengthen, counsel, and pray for one another. They are told to "Be sober, be watchful. Your adversary the devil prowls around like a roaring lion, seeking some one to devour" (1 Peter 5:8-9).

Living in Christ means understanding who Satan is and believing that the message of Scripture about Satan is meant to be taken seriously and at face value. The Bible says: "The whole world is in the power of the evil one" (1 John 5:19). Satan snatches away the implanted truth of the gospel (Matthew 13:19), is "the deceiver of the whole world" (Revelation 12:9), is able to counterfeit what is the genuine power of God (Acts 8:9-11), is a tempter (Luke 22:31), can cause physical illness (Luke 13:16), blinds men spiritually (2 Corinthians 4:4); and some under the control of Satan, like the possessed girl in Acts 16:16, are seemingly willing to promote the ministry of Christ. But the Scriptures also make clear that Jesus Christ triumphs over Satan: "I saw Satan fall like lightning from heaven" (Luke 10:18).

Living in Christ also means sharing Christ. The church as the body of believers is equipped to do this. Every newspaper article, every magazine, and every book that tell of even one more person going into the occult serve as calls to obey the Great Commission. The motive for obedience is not some silly fear that "we might be overrun." Christians are past caring about their own well-being. They obey because a disciple always obeys his master and because of an overwhelming desire to share with another valuable human being the life-giving love of Jesus.

Living in Christ also means worshiping him through a total yielding of ourselves to him. Worship goes beyond lip service and Sunday mornings. It includes the daily awareness of God in our lives and the listening to him through prayer and Scripture. Worship keeps the Christian reminded that he is not his own, he has been "bought with a price." The gathering of believers on Sunday says to the world today what it said to the world of the first century, "The Lord is risen."

Living in Christ keeps the Christian from being afraid. Satan will work on Christians, just as he worked on Jesus. But the surrounding strength of Christ is the strength of one who is God and cannot be overcome. This strength brings a comforting feeling and it gives a comforting peace.

The Christian church at this moment in history has a great opportunity to teach, to love, to heal, and to liberate those who have been caught in the forces controlled by Satan. Although an ever-increasing number of people are being captured and bound, the church of Jesus Christ has the means and the message to set people free.

SETTING PEOPLE FREE

"They came day and night, never giving me up," wrote a girl in the *Hollywood Free Paper,* telling how the Christians had helped her get free of the occult.

She was "tripping" out of her body through astral projection. One day, she had the frightening experience of getting her soul outside of her body and not being able to return. She was on the ceiling of her room, trying to reach her body on the bed and couldn't get to it. After that experience, she went through weeks of agony as the Christians kept coming back to help her, and she struggled between their prayers and her old master. She described the battle as someone holding the corner of her soul and pulling in the opposite direction. She did give herself to Christ and has been free from the control of the occult for more than two years.

"I was looking for the soul side of life. That's why I got into satanism," explained an ex-Satan worshiper who is now enrolled in a theological seminary to prepare for the Christian ministry.

"Two things shocked me," he said. "One was the realization that the so-called Christian establishment had not accepted God and was not Christian, and I could no longer use them as an example of hypocrisy; and the second was hearing that Jesus is coming again and I would someday have to meet him.

"When I met head-on the claims of Christ that were biblically presented to me, there began a struggle in me that almost tore me apart. It was like being on a spiritual battleground. I actually felt the power of God fighting against the power of Satan inside of me. A few days later I came to Christ."

Satan does not let people go easily. There is a war going on in the person reaching for Christ, and it is not easily won. A Christian pastor, who was once in the occult himself, says it takes patience and understanding to be able to minister to demonized people and to bring them out of it. The Christian who is helping must overlook what the demon-possessed person says and does, not arguing with him but clarifying for him what exorcism of the demon through Christ means.

Christians need to be very careful at this point. One young Christian, zealous to liberate everyone from the grip of Satan, went around commanding Satan to "come out of this person." He soon was creating a lot of problems. He never identified the demon or had the person involved identify the demon. He never asked the possessed person to articulate for himself what deliverance he wanted. He was so intent on deciding who was possessed and proving how good he was as an exorcist that he did a lot of harm.

Quiet, prayerful concern, couched in biblical wisdom and love, and tempered with the willingness to let God do his own work, will enable Christians to help many move away from Satan's grasp. But when Satan does possess a person so that he is demonized, exorcism is necessary. The work of exorcism, having been shelved for many years, is being examined again as a necessary work of the church. In England, the ancient, but neglected, practice of exorcism has been revived by the Church of England to counter the spread of witchcraft.

The Christian needs to be alert to possible physical and mental disorders that require medical care, but he should realize, too, that some of the problems written off as "mental illness" may be demon possession, which of course does affect the mind. Paul Tournier, the Swiss physician and psychiatrist, has commented that Christian confession can be as freeing as some of the best psychoanalytical care. Some have found that where exorcism is needed, psychotherapy does not bring relief. A demon-possessed person has to *know* that Jesus has set him free. Exorcism calls out the demon in the name and by the authority of Jesus Christ. He alone is the victor over Satan and can loose a person trapped by him. Jesus did this while he was on this earth, and many exorcists are finding that he is doing it again today.

Freeing a person requires three steps, the first of which is confession. The person with a demon needs to confess what it is that has him bound. If he has made a pact with Satan, or has been involved with the spirits or the tarot or the Ouija board, he must confess it. Praying with a person has little meaning if he is not willing to identify before God what it is that he needs to have taken out of his life. In some instances people do not even know what it is that holds them. It is important to ask a troubled person if he has ever been involved in psychic games or experiences, even innocently as a child. One Christian missionary had been plagued with a feeling that she could not identify, but which was crippling her witness. With the help of other Christians she recalled an experience as a child when her mother involved her in seances. Identifying it and turning the burden over to God gave her a real sense of liberation and peace.

A dying man was in agony over what he called a demon in him. He kept pleading with his family to take his demon. Not believing in demons and concerned to calm him, one relative said, "I'll take your demon." The man calmed down, but in the weeks following, the one who took the demon began experiencing the same symptoms of possession. Possession is real and can happen to anyone who opens himself up to it.

Secondly, having identified and confessed the demon, the possessed person needs to renounce the demon in the name of Jesus. He, or those praying for him, must call out the demon that is binding him by the name and authority of Jesus. All ownership of the demon is denied and the ownership of Jesus is confessed.

Even though the disciples had power over demons in Jesus' name (Luke 10:17), some Christians today still have trouble believing that Jesus can cast out demons. They prefer to see the problem as a psychological one. Demons do affect people psychologically, but the problem is spiritual and whatever psychological treatment that is needed and given should not exclude the renunciation of the demon. Verbal renunciation of the demon and confession of Jesus do bring healing. When we understand the full meaning of the redemptive process, this result is not startling.

The third step is assurance or absolution. The freed person needs to know on the authority of God's word that he is delivered. This step is no different than showing a person that confessing Christ as Savior does in fact make salvation his. He should be shown that he has been delivered by the power of God and can live by the indwelling presence of God. There are many illustrations in Scripture of people being liberated from demons. A person can be shown that God does not change. He has called, and God has answered. He has been set at liberty by the liberating Christ who has the authority to do so.

The person who is being exorcised must confess and renounce

every part of Satan's grip and every demon that holds him. Otherwise there could still be demons plaguing him, even after he has confessed one or more. This process may take some time, even several different periods of prayer. Left with a demon and the door open, his last state could be worse than the first. Other demons will come in, given the opportunity. Jesus said that they would (Matthew 12:43-45).

The exorcist should know the difference between demon possession and being demonized. Demons do plague people but that is different than possession. Possession is the actual moving in and taking over a life. Christian counselor Kurt E. Koch has written several books on demonism with many cases of people vexed through involvement in occultism. [3] He illustrates different forms of possession including those in which people aren't even aware of what the demon in them is doing or saying.

Satan moves into a life in many ways. He may send several evil spirits. To pray about one spirit may still leave the possessed person with others. Jesus illustrated the capacity of Satan to fill a person when he freed the man with legions of demons. The person exorcised must ask Jesus Christ to fill him, replacing all of the demons, or they could rush in again to fill the void.

Praying with a demon-possessed person takes understanding, patience, and love. Some feel that exorcism is not a church matter. "It is very private," said one pastor who has an extensive ministry in exorcism, "just as surgery is very private." He explained that some of the actions of the demon are embarrassing to the person after he is freed. Strange compulsions, blanking out, voices not their own swearing or insulting, and other physical and mental torments should be handled privately and with discretion. It is not a public affair.

Others feel that exorcism is definitely a matter for the whole Christian fellowship. The praying of many people, the laying on of hands, and the strength of numbers is beneficial. The presence of others also insures that the exorcist is not overpowered by the demon or that he begins to think of himself as the miracle worker. Whether done publicly or privately, the surgical analogy is a good one; exorcism is a very serious, personal matter.

[3] Most of Kurt E. Koch's books are in German, but *Christian Counseling and Occultism* and *The Devil's Alphabet* are available in English translations through Kregal Publications, of Grand Rapids.

Christians praying for a demon-possessed person must be very careful that the real problem is articulated. Some people want to be freed from the torments of demon possession but do not want to be freed from the demon itself. The demon gives them power and some pleasure, even as it owns them.

Experience shows that drugs, mental illness, or any other problem that can be used or manipulated by Satan is not the same as being possessed. Getting rid of the problem does not get rid of Satan. The testimony of a street Christian, published in *The Jesus Kids*, illustrates the difference:

> It wasn't hard to get off drugs and sex, but my former friends had put the curse of Satan on me. I used to be into Satan with them, and it was hard to get away. It was getting me down because I was wearing myself out trying to fight what was too much for me. Alone, I was incapable of handling the power that Satan had over me. I had to trust the Lord because he had already overcome Satan. I knew that Satan couldn't win against him.[4]

Christian exorcism of demons is not a game or some spiritual jag. It is very serious business. The whole church has the responsibility of knowing who is practicing exorcism. Exorcism is not for the spiritually immature. There are, unfortunately, people running around calling themselves exorcists and causing serious problems to the ministry of the church and hurting the people who need help.

The Christian exorcist stands on holy ground. He knows that the Lord, not the exorcist, frees a demon-possessed person. He works with fear and humility, knowing that for his own reasons, God has chosen to use him. He works in harmony with the church, and always for the sake of others.

When a person has committed his heart and life to Jesus Christ and has asked Jesus to possess him, then he will not dabble in the occult. He serves the one true God. Neither will he have to fear the control of Satan, only the temptation to submit. But he must consciously determine to follow Christ, daily looking to him for strength. In a day of sweeping occultism, there is no room for a casual Christian stand.

Christ is the victor. He has seen Satan fall. In the dawning of the Age of Aquarius, Christians committed to Christ and his redemptive power stand as islands of rescue in a very rough sea. They are

[4] Roger C. Palms, *The Jesus Kids* (Valley Forge: Judson Press, 1971), p. 19.

like beacons of light on a dark night calling the demon possessed to wholeness, offering a hand of help as the disciples did so long ago.

The living, reigning Christ has called for obedience and has empowered his disciples in a way that only he could describe: ". . . I say to you, he who believes in me will also do the works that I do; and greater works than these will he do, because I go to the Father" (John 14:12).

Jesus has come to give life and to give it abundantly. The Christian is called today to live what he *is* in Christ and to share what he *has* in Christ. And in the dark occult night of the Aquarian Age, the Light will shine in the darkness, and Satan will not be able to put it out.

Author's Postscript

"Do you realize what you are doing?" That question was asked again and again by concerned Christians as I traveled and researched and interviewed. They feared that Satan would hurt me or my family in an effort to block the work on *The Christian and the Occult.*

They knew, as I knew, that Satan is real and has more power to hurt than most of us realize. But two things were certain as I began my work: I knew that the book needed to be written, and I knew that I needed the prayer support of fellow Christians.

So I answered my concerned friends by assuring them that I had thought and prayed very seriously about what I was doing and that Christians all over the country were supporting me with prayer. And always the concerned Christians would reply, "Well, we are praying for you, too."

There were some spiritually low times during the writing when I felt that Satan was closing in. But then my students, who followed the development of this book, would pray more earnestly for me—even putting their arms around me or taking my hands to let me have that spiritual contact.

So the writing of *The Christian and the Occult* became a deeply meaningful spiritual experience. One special moment stands out above many others. I was standing in front of Anton LaVey's black house talking to one of his neighbors. It was a beautiful warm Saturday afternoon. The spring sky was clear, except for a few white clouds. As I looked up past LaVey's roof, I was overwhelmed with the feeling "God is right here!" There, next to a place where

Satan is worshiped, was the all-encompassing beauty of God.

As I reflected on this and started to think about the hundreds of people who were praying for me, I was so warmly filled that the street became for me a place of worship. How great it is to belong to God and the church and to know the indescribably beautiful nearness of Christ!

I share this experience, because I fear that someone reading *The Christian and the Occult* might think it would be fun to "check out" a few occult activities for himself, not having the prayer support that I had. I urge you not to do it. Instead, find just one person who has met Jesus Christ after being in the occult. He will tell you why, from firsthand experience, you should resist the occult and not go anywhere near it. You will not be less effective as a Christian witness for not having some firsthand occult experiences. Jesus didn't have such experiences either, but he understood the power of Satan. Stay close to Jesus.